Euthanasia

Other Books of Related Interest

Euthanasia

Lisa Yount, *Book Editor*

Daniel Leone, *President*
Bonnie Szumski, *Publisher*
Scott Barbour, *Managing Editor*
Brenda Stalcup, *Series Editor*

Contemporary Issues
Companion

Greenhaven Press, Inc., San Diego, CA

Every effort has been made to trace the owners of copyrighted material. The articles in this volume may have been edited for content, length, and/or reading level. The titles have been changed to enhance the editorial purpose. Those interested in locating the original source will find the complete citation on the first page of each article.

Library of Congress Cataloging-in-Publication Data

Euthanasia / Lisa Yount, book editor.
    p. cm. — (Contemporary issues companion)
    Includes bibliographical references and index.
    ISBN 0-7377-0828-X (pbk. : alk. paper) —
ISBN 0-7377-0829-8 (lib. : alk. paper)
    1. Euthanasia. 2. Euthanasia—Moral and ethical aspects.
3. Medical ethics. I. Yount, Lisa. II. Series.

R726 .E782 2002
179.7—dc21

179.7
E

c.1

2001033778
CIP

© 2002 by Greenhaven Press, Inc.
P.O. Box 289009, San Diego, CA 92198-9009

Printed in the U.S.A.

CONTENTS

FOREWORD

In the news, on the streets, and in neighborhoods, individuals are confronted with a variety of social problems. Such problems may affect people directly: A young woman may struggle with depression, suspect a friend of having bulimia, or watch a loved one battle cancer. And even the issues that do not directly affect her private life—such as religious cults, domestic violence, or legalized gambling—still impact the larger society in which she lives. Discovering and analyzing the complexities of issues that encompass communal and societal realms as well as the world of personal experience is a valuable educational goal in the modern world.

Effectively addressing social problems requires familiarity with a constantly changing stream of data. Becoming well informed about today's controversies is an intricate process that often involves reading myriad primary and secondary sources, analyzing political debates, weighing various experts' opinions—even listening to first-hand accounts of those directly affected by the issue. For students and general observers, this can be a daunting task because of the sheer volume of information available in books, periodicals, on the evening news, and on the Internet. Researching the consequences of legalized gambling, for example, might entail sifting through congressional testimony on gambling's societal effects, examining private studies on Indian gaming, perusing numerous websites devoted to Internet betting, and reading essays written by lottery winners as well as interviews with recovering compulsive gamblers. Obtaining valuable information can be time-consuming—since it often requires researchers to pore over numerous documents and commentaries before discovering a source relevant to their particular investigation.

Greenhaven's Contemporary Issues Companion series seeks to assist this process of research by providing readers with useful and pertinent information about today's complex issues. Each volume in this anthology series focuses on a topic of current interest, presenting informative and thought-provoking selections written from a wide variety of viewpoints. The readings selected by the editors include such diverse sources as personal accounts and case studies, pertinent factual and statistical articles, and relevant commentaries and overviews. This diversity of sources and views, found in every Contemporary Issues Companion, offers readers a broad perspective in one convenient volume.

In addition, each title in the Contemporary Issues Companion series is designed especially for young adults. The selections included in every volume are chosen for their accessibility and are expertly edited in consideration of both the reading and comprehension levels of the audience. The structure of the anthologies also enhances accessibility. An introductory essay places each issue in context and provides helpful facts such as historical background or current statistics and legislation that pertain to the topic. The chapters that follow organize the material and focus on specific aspects of the book's topic. Every essay is introduced by a brief summary of its main points and biographical information about the author. These summaries aid in comprehension and can also serve to direct readers to material of immediate interest and need. Finally, a comprehensive index allows readers to efficiently scan and locate content.

The Contemporary Issues Companion series is an ideal launching point for research on a particular topic. Each anthology in the series is composed of readings taken from an extensive gamut of resources, including periodicals, newspapers, books, government documents, the publications of private and public organizations, and Internet websites. In these volumes, readers will find factual support suitable for use in reports, debates, speeches, and research papers. The anthologies also facilitate further research, featuring a book and periodical bibliography and a list of organizations to contact for additional information.

A perfect resource for both students and the general reader, Greenhaven's Contemporary Issues Companion series is sure to be a valued source of current, readable information on social problems that interest young adults. It is the editors' hope that readers will find the Contemporary Issues Companion series useful as a starting point to formulate their own opinions about and answers to the complex issues of the present day.

INTRODUCTION

The meaning of the phrase "right to die" has already changed once. In the 1970s and 1980s, when this issue was first discussed extensively, the term chiefly meant the right of people (or their families, if they were incompetent) to refuse life-sustaining medical treatment. The New Jersey Supreme Court's decision in the case of Karen Ann Quinlan in 1976 and the U.S. Supreme Court's ruling in the case of Nancy Cruzan in 1990 affirmed that United States citizens had a constitutional right to refuse any form of medical treatment (a right actually established in a 1914 court decision). Further, it was held that surrogates had the right to refuse treatment, including food and water, on behalf of incompetent people provided that those people had left clear evidence of their wishes while competent.

With the question of treatment refusal settled in the minds of most, in the 1990s the phrase "right to die" came to refer to a more controversial form of hastened death: physician-assisted suicide. Right-to-die supporters claimed that terminally ill people (generally defined as those expected to die within six months) should be permitted to ask a physician for assistance in suicide, usually in the form of a prescription for a lethal drug. The Supreme Court ruled in 1997 that no such right could be inferred from the U.S. Constitution. However, the court left the door open for individual states to legalize physician-assisted suicide. One state, Oregon, has done so.

Many among both advocates and adversaries of physician-assisted suicide and its even more hotly debated cousin, euthanasia,* believe that within the next 10 or 20 years the focus of right-to-die discussions will change again. The question, they say, will become not whether a terminally or seriously ill person has a right to die but whether such a person has a duty to die. The forces that will bring about this change, they predict, are the aging of the population in developed countries and the continuing attempt to control the costs of health care in those same countries.

Thanks to the miracles of medical technology and improvements in the standard of living, people in countries like the United States are living longer than ever. The average life expectancy in the United States is in the year 2000 76.1 years, and those over 85 years old are the fastest growing segment of the country's population. Yet an unfortunate side effect of this admirable growth in longevity is that more people are suffering from chronic (long-lasting) illnesses, which disproportionately strike the elderly. An increase in chronic illness, in

---

*Euthanasia: When someone other than the patient, usually a physician, performs the lethal act; this word is also sometimes used to refer to all forms of aid in dying.

turn, is one of the factors predicted to continue driving up the cost of health care. Long-term care for such illnesses was estimated to cost $123 billion yearly in 2000, and that figure was expected to nearly triple by 2040 to a staggering $346 billion.

A desire to halt steeply rising health care costs in the 1980s and early 1990s gave rise to health maintenance organizations (HMOs) and other forms of managed care in the United States. These organizations pay for, monitor, and provide health care. They controlled costs chiefly by limiting care, especially expensive care. At the same time, faced with similar cost problems, government-run health care systems such as Britain's National Health Service also began to limit some kinds of care. These actions eliminated much waste and dangerous overtreatment, such as unnecessary X-rays and operations. However, critics claim that they also denied some treatments that physicians deemed beneficial or even essential for their patients' health.

As demands on health care systems continue to increase, it is hard to predict how far such limitations will go. "We're talking about cutting Medicare [the government-sponsored program that pays for health care for the elderly in the United States] and our social obligation to take care of the disabled, and at the same time we're also talking about physician-assisted suicide, and no one's noticing that they might come together in a very difficult way," warns Joanne Lynn, a specialist in the care of the elderly. Lynn and other opponents of assisted suicide fear that if growing numbers of the sick, disabled, and elderly are denied care that could help them maintain comfort and independence, they might be tempted to take their own lives.

Strikingly, some supporters of assisted suicide and euthanasia say that such a development might not be an entirely bad thing. Derek Humphry and Mary Clement, co-authors of the 1998 book *Freedom to Die: People, Politics and the Right-to-Die Movement*, wrote:

> A new study of seriously ill people in hospitals found that 30 percent of those surveyed said they would rather *die* than live permanently in a nursing home. . . . Why do we, as a nation, not allow these people to die . . . ? Their lives would conclude with dignity and self-respect, and one measure of cost containment would be in place.

Given the fact that a single lethal dose of medication costs considerably less than months or years of high-tech care, opponents of assisted suicide and euthanasia are concerned that if these practices ever become widespread, financially strapped health care organizations may pressure physicians to recommend hastened death, just as they now often pressure doctors to deny care. In a respected 1997 report, the New York Task Force on Life and the Law concluded that "assisted suicide . . . is just too cheap relative to the available medical alternatives [for treating disability or chronic illness]. . . . In a world of market medicine and tightening government budgets, cheap is all too likely to mean attractive." Some critics even fear that governments might force euthanasia on people, as the Nazis did between 1939 and 1941 in a program that killed some 100,000 mentally or physically disabled Germans.

Supporters of physician-assisted suicide and euthanasia say that the risk of forced or coerced death can be minimized. Martin Gunderson and David J. Mayo, for example, recommend limiting legal physician-assisted suicide to the terminally ill for this reason. Others claim that safeguards like those in the Oregon law, such as a requirement for two clear requests to die with a waiting period in between, can prevent most cases of coercion. These existing safeguards could be further strengthened by adding a requirement for mandatory psychiatric evaluation for depression or for provision of appropriate palliative ("comfort") care such as pain relief.

Supporters also claim that the right to discontinue medical care could be abused just as easily as the right to ask for suicide or euthanasia, yet there is little evidence that this has occurred. Similarly, they point to the small number of legal assisted suicides reported by the Oregon Health Division as evidence that widespread abuse is not occurring. However, opponents such as Kathleen Foley and Herbert Hendin claim that the Health Division's reports depend too much on the word of physicians rather than patients. Hendin, furthermore, reports that in the Netherlands, the only country where assisted suicide and euthanasia are both legal (as of 2001) and widely practiced, physicians have apparently carried out euthanasia on competent patients who have not requested it.

Most people on both sides of the right-to-die debate believe that if legalization of physician-assisted suicide and euthanasia takes place at all, it must be handled very carefully in order to prevent the right to die from becoming a duty to die. Options in facing death and caring for the dying must be discussed clearly, without excessive emotion or namecalling. As Thomas A. Shannon, Professor of Religion and Social Ethics at the Worcester Polytechnic Institute in Massachusetts, has said:

> The prolonged public debate served to clarify the issues and helped establish a national consensus which supported the removal of therapies that prolonged life but provided few other benefits. . . . The nation benefited because there was no fast resolution [of this debate]. . . . Only a genuine national, popular debate can benefit the resolution of this issue [the desirability of physician-assisted suicide and euthanasia].

The questions of whether hastened death might be abused and how possible abuse might be prevented are just two of the topics addressed in *Euthanasia: Contemporary Issues Companion*. The book also places euthanasia (including physician-assisted suicide) in the context of end-of-life care as a whole and provides information and pro-and-con opinions concerning physicians' role in hastening death, euthanasia and the law, euthanasia in practice, and the ethics of euthanasia. As longevity increases and growing numbers of people must face chronic and debilitating illness and death in themselves or their loved ones, the many questions raised by the idea of hastened death are sure to become more pressing. Burke Balch, director of medical ethics at the National Right to Life Committee, says, "There is no question that the struggle over euthanasia will be one of the most dominant issues into the [twenty-first] century."

CHAPTER 1

FACING THE END OF LIFE

TECHNOLOGY CAN MAKE DEATH HARD

Ginny Cunningham

Medical technology saves many lives, says Ginny Cunningham, but it can also make dying a lengthy and torturous process. As a result, some dying people or their families ask to stop medical treatment, even though death may result. Honest talks with family members and advance directives stating a person's wishes for end-of-life care can help to ensure that those wishes will be followed, Cunningham explains. She says that if people face their fear of death with "faithful self-possession," they can reap spiritual rewards. Cunningham has written several articles for *U.S. Catholic* and is the author of *The Spirituality of Work: Military Personnel.*

"It's stupid to say I want to know why," says June Russo, 68, who stood helpless at her 38-year-old daughter's bedside in August 1995 while Chrissy's organs shut down and blood gushed from her eyes. "But I can't put it aside yet."

Afflicted by a rare genetic condition that had already taken the lives of three members of the extended family, all five Russo children were checked regularly for symptomatic polyps. When Chrissy, the middle child, was 16, she was diagnosed as having a mutant variation of the condition that blanketed her organs with hundreds of polyps. Surgery provided relief. For 12 years Chrissy was relatively symptom free. She married. Then pregnancy seemed to trigger a recurrence and the beginning of a long downhill slide that began with the loss of the twins she carried.

In 1992, Chrissy lay dying at Beth Israel Hospital in New York City, not far from her New Jersey home. One of her doctors suggested an intestinal transplant, something the Russos weren't aware was an option. Though intestinal transplantation was highly experimental, it offered what seemed Chrissy's only hope for life. "We talked, and Chrissy agreed to it," June recalls, pinpointing the moment of choice "where it all started."

Chrissy, whose husband had abandoned her when her health deteriorated, was flown to the University of Pittsburgh Medical Center.

"She came through the transplant," June says. But the family spent the next 2½ years in limbo. Chrissy received countless blood transfusions and repeated surgeries that cost her insurance company more than $1 million, in addition to costs related to transplantation that were covered by research funds.

"We knew it was experimental surgery, but it was tragic from the beginning," June says. "At the end, she had raging infections; none of the medication was doing any good. She was on oxygen and dialysis [treatment to clean the blood after kidneys have failed]. Her organs were going one by one. It was so bad." As June talks about the unrelieved stress of those years, she admits "the anger is killing me."

Technological Dilemmas

Nothing could have spared June and her husband Michael the suffering that parents endure when they witness the death of a child they have raised. But today advanced medical technologies compound this suffering in ways that earlier generations were spared and that families are ill equipped to cope with. Worse, families will make some of the most important decisions of their lives about what technology to use and how to use it while desperately anxious about loved ones and relatively ignorant of the technology's fine points and potential effects—for good and ill. They're not likely to have living wills or other advance directives—fewer than 15 percent of Americans do. They'll turn to a chaplain or pastoral-care person, expecting answers and insights, as well as solace, only to find that medical technology has outstripped any merely human capacity to clearly define appropriate action in every scenario.

Is the dilemma that medical technology presents in end-of-life situations one that can be resolved? Drawing on ancient and contemporary Christian tradition, theologians and ethicists have developed wise and insightful guidelines for medical situations when decisions must be made about the use of advanced technologies.

But is the dilemma essentially technological, or is the contemporary medical setting merely one of this century's settings for our most ancient and intimate struggle with our vulnerability, our humanity, and our mortality?

As Daniel Callahan, president and cofounder of the Hastings Center and distinguished medical-ethics expert, says in his book *The Troubled Dream of Life: In Search of a Peaceful Death* (Georgetown University Press), modern medicine appeals

> to our hopes and our desires as much as to our minds. . . . [its power] resides in its almost magical possibility of offering us a relief from biological necessity, granting us new powers to manage our fate and our destiny, presenting an image of unlimited hope, genuine knowledge, and great progress. It assumes the possibility of dominating, manipulating, and

redefining nature and its potencies. This is a powerful and compelling image to a self all too conscious of its fragility.

On one hand, it seems the medical community is to blame for much of the problem. Doctors traditionally associate death with defeat. They're poorly trained, if trained at all, in bedside manner for dying patients. Studies show that even training in the kind of pain management that could alleviate [ease] apprehension about the dying process is sorely lacking. What physicians can offer are seemingly endless choices that allow them to defer or elude the moment when there's nothing else to offer.

But patients and families themselves are often as ill prepared to arrive at that moment, says David F. Kelly, professor of theology and medical ethics and director of the Center for Health Care at Duquesne University in Pittsburgh and hospital ethicist at Saint Francis Medical Center in Pittsburgh. "For every case where doctors offer endless choices," he says, "I can tell you of a case where a family wouldn't let go and demanded more."

Advance Directives

As director of the Department of Pastoral Care at University of Pittsburgh Medical Center, a massive hospital conglomerate that is known internationally for its transplantation, cardiology, orthopedics, oncology, and general medicine, Father Sam Esposito sees it all.

It's not unusual, he says, for patients to find themselves on a conveyor of what is actually extraordinary care that they have every right to refuse. But they may not know that.

Catholic ethicists, such as Sister Jean deBlois, C.S.J. [Congregation of Saint Joseph] and Rev. Kevin D. Cyrourke, O.P. [Order of Preachers], J.C.D. [Doctor of Civil Law], who have written about Ethical and Religious Directives (ERD) for Catholic Health Care Services, date the use of the terms ordinary or extraordinary to the 17th century and stress that the terms make ethical and moral, rather than medical, distinctions. What is considered ordinary for a person who has a decent chance of recovery might well be extraordinary for a person whose chance of recovery is less. Ideally that decision would be made by the individual, and often it is.

Catholic tradition demands only that ordinary means—that offer reasonable hope of benefit and are not an excessive burden on the patient—be taken to preserve life.

To prepare for such an event, many people prepare advance directives, in the form of a living will or a durable power of attorney for health care. The first and most important thing that advance directives do, Kelly says, is get people talking to each other about what they want if they become incompetent. Sometimes, talking is enough.

Pat Fenton, 50, was with his mother, brother, sister, in-laws, aunts, and uncles at his 91-year-old father's bedside last summer, allowing the family patriarch to die. Months earlier, Pat says, his father had been rushed to the hospital, where doctors insisted that he would die without immediate surgery. "Dad refused surgery and was back home within two days." But in July, the family was faced with a similar situation. "Dad was no longer conscious; but because he had told us a few months earlier that he didn't want surgery," Pat says, "we knew we should reject that option." Even though the family didn't have a written directive, they had a strong sense of the patient's wishes, and those wishes had been expressed recently enough to be credible to attending health-care professionals.

Advance directives address a competent patient's constitutional right to refuse medical treatment, including artificial nutrition and hydration [food and liquids], but different forms of directives address different functions. A living will, signed by an individual and a witness, can give direction about treatments to administer or withhold if you are incompetent and about termination of life support.

A durable power of attorney for health care appoints someone to make medical decisions on your behalf and only comes into play if you are incompetent.

Advance directives are compatible with Catholic theology and ERD for Catholic Health Care Services and urge avoiding two extremes: "an insistence on useless or burdensome technology even when a patient may legitimately wish to forgo it and, on the other hand, the withdrawal of technology with the intention of causing death."

Deciding to Say No

But what if a patient is already on life support and will die if life support is removed? ERD states that "death occurs because a fatal pathological condition is allowed to take its natural course, not because those who have removed life support intended to kill the patient. Rather, their intention is to stop doing something useless or to stop imposing a burden on the patient."

On the day that Pat's family refused surgery for his dad, they also had to make a decision about medication. The elderly man was in extreme pain, but administering the dosage of medication necessary to alleviate the pain would suppress the man's respiration and hasten his death. Should the medication be administered anyway?

Guided by a certain sense of inevitability, the family nodded agreement. ERD would have concurred. "Medicines capable of alleviating or suppressing pain may be given to a dying person even if this therapy may indirectly shorten the person's life so long as the intent is not to hasten death."

"Catholic tradition is pretty balanced on these issues," Callahan says, even though there is mixed opinion about the use of feeding tubes. Some U.S. bishops and a minority of Catholic theologians, wary of a slippery slope toward euthanasia, take a position toward artificial nutrition and hydration that is even more conservative than is advocated by ERD.

Callahan suggests that such positions encourage rather than discourage tolerance of euthanasia, which, according to every recent study, is on the increase. "People don't want useless, futile treatment and ultra-conservative statements generate fear that the medical community won't be allowed to give up on them."

Are advance directives adequate response to advanced medical technologies and the agonizing choices they can present, as well as a guarantee of death with dignity?

"Advance directives are quite helpful, but not in the way people think," Kelly says. "If people think they will solve the matter and eliminate complexity, they don't." On the contrary, "they can advance the sense that we are in control of absolutely everything, and we simply are not."

The primary benefit of a proxy directive—a durable power of attorney—is to help avoid imposing an overly heavy burden on loved ones.

Theologically, naming a proxy is less an act of "control" than an indication of trust. "You're acknowledging that you will not have control and that you have to trust someone," Kelly says. "Advance directives give some level of control over who decides, but that control is based on trust."

On the other hand, living wills, especially those that contain detailed, explicit instruction about many levels of treatment, foster a sense of solving a problem, Kelly says, when, in practice, the situations they describe "almost never happen."

What we need to pay attention to in living wills, he says, is the underlying message: "please don't do stupid stuff to me. Nobody wants stuff done for them that isn't going to do any good."

Helping a Loved One

Jesuit-trained Jerry Voros has considered every possible health-care decision that he will be forced to make for his wife Carla, who has been bedridden for four years, almost completely paralyzed and unable to communicate. A tube that was inserted to enable her breathing rendered her speechless, and severe palsy prevents her from writing or even using block letters to express herself.

Jerry has completed and filed a living will and durable power of attorney for health care—he keeps a copy at home, with Carla's physician, and with the hospital where Carla is most likely to be treated. But Jerry's sense of control seems no greater than June Russo's.

Carla was only 51 when she began having problems with depth perception and began tripping and falling. Her youngest son, 15-year-old Matthew, remarked to Jerry about Mom's "terrible driving," but, Jerry, busy with his job as president of Ketchum Communications, missed or dismissed symptoms.

Ultimately, Carla's instability was attributed to an incurable degeneration of the cerebellum that would incapacitate her. By the time she was 60, Carla was confined to a wheelchair and had trouble swallowing.

Today Carla spends her days on an air mattress in a hospital bed set up in the living room of the city apartment she and Jerry occupy. Retired now, Jerry helps care for Carla, but except for the one or two midnight shifts each week when he keeps watch alone, nurses are constantly present, turning Carla, reading to her, and talking to her about their lives, even though she can't respond.

Carla is probably alive only because of the seemingly extraordinary care that Jerry is able to provide. Without it, any complication would have killed her. But is it a life that can or should be lengthened?

There was a time when Jerry and Carla might have said no. They agreed that Carla would never be placed on an artificial respirator. Nevertheless, the need arose while Jerry was on a business trip, and Carla was rushed to the hospital and diagnosed with pneumonia. "They just did it," he says. He pauses. "Some would have pulled the respirator. That would have been a loss to me. I don't know what it would have been to Carla. At times like that, your desire to live outweighs any consideration of how you will live."

In a voice tinged with humor rather than regret or self-pity, Jerry describes the home he retired to: filled with people he wouldn't necessarily choose to have around all the time and a life with no privacy.

"To me, there is no alternative to caring for my wife," he says. "We are social beings. We must help each other." But without Carla, the stabilizing fabric of Jerry's life would be gone, he says. "It's frightening to think of being alone. What would I be doing if I wasn't doing this?"

Preparing for the End of Life

Should Chrissy and her family have accepted so many treatments and fought so hard for almost three years? Would it have been less painful in the end, cheaper, and theologically acceptable if Chrissy had been allowed to die sooner?

"You can ask yourself till you're green," June Russo says. "It bought her three years. The quality was bad. But it was life. She never faltered. She accepted those years and never complained. How can I?"

Advanced medical technologies sorely test our capacity to make wise choices—whether to refuse or accept treatment, and how to weigh benefits and burdens. Esposito suggests that a new American tradition would help: "Talking at the Thanksgiving dinner table about what we would want."

"People need to talk to each other about what they would want," Esposito says. "This shouldn't be something that you look at for the first time when a family member's been in the I.C.U. [intensive care unit] for 145 days and a social worker walks in to talk about options."

Ideally people will prepare, Kelly says. "Spiritually: pray a lot. Financially: get your affairs in order. Medically: name a proxy, and tell that person what you would want. Make out a general living will; talk this over with your family and your physician."

Whether or not we are prepared, end-of-life issues have the greatest potential for throwing us headlong and fully armed with denial into face-to-face conflict with our deeply lurking terror of what we do not know and cannot control.

But within that darkness is an invitation to explore freedom that is not grounded in a capacity to control, and the chance to choose faithful self-possession that redeems what it cannot change.

"Fragility is our human condition," Callahan writes. "To attempt to remove that sense of threat once and for all, to intimate to another that such suffering need not be borne, is to cut the very soul out of human life."

Our spiritual task remains to look unblinking at the fearful people that we are and to relinquish the power we only thought that we had. In that act is our dignity and grace.

ON THE FRONT LINES WITH DEATH

Jennifer Hunter

Palliative care, or comfort care, is given to people whose illnesses cannot be cured. In this selection, Jennifer Hunter, a regular writer for the Canadian newsmagazine *Maclean's*, describes the daily work of Doris De Groot, a specialist in palliative care. Hunter explains that De Groot does more than make sure that pain and other physical problems are controlled. She also "helps people die," Hunter says, by guiding patients and their families to face the emotional agony of this difficult time. Hunter notes that De Groot does not condone physician-assisted suicide, but she respects dying patients' decisions to end their own lives.

Doris De Groot helps people die. A palliative care physician in Vancouver, Canada, De Groot works with patients in their last weeks or months of life, making them as comfortable and pain-free as she can. "To do what I do," says the doctor, "you have to be able to walk into a situation where there is a lot of emotion, a lot of grief, and feel that you can create something positive out of it." Her job is not just to help a patient deal with pain. "You're helping them and their family come to terms with death," says De Groot.

Palliative care workers—doctors, nurses, social workers, ministers—often step in when there is no other medical solution for patients. Most have cancer or AIDS, but some are dying from heart or lung problems or other causes. Yet De Groot finds her job much more spiritually uplifting than psychologically draining. Death, says the 42-year-old physician, is part of living, an experience emotionally akin to birth. "With the right support," she affirms, "a family can experience growth and healing in the dying process."

Easing the Pain of Dying

De Groot is part of a team working for the health board of Vancouver and neighboring Richmond. Her day typically starts with a rash of phone calls and pager beeps demanding immediate response. A home-care nurse's patient is not coping well with pain; a family doctor is not sure what medication to prescribe; a despondent cancer sufferer is contemplating suicide. "Sometimes," she says, "a family doctor will phone and say 'I'm over my head, can you come and help?'" Family physicians do not always know how to alleviate a dying person's symptoms. Nurses cannot write prescriptions and do not always know how to negotiate their way through the medical system. So De Groot finds the equipment a patient needs. She frequently phones pharmacists and arranges for taxis to pick up prescriptions. She decides whether pain medication should be changed from oral dosages to a subcutaneous [under the skin] drip, and if the dosage should be increased.

The support teams also include the patient's family doctor, a clinical nurse specialist, a social worker and a volunteer co-ordinator who sends non-paid, sympathetic "listeners" to the patients' homes to spell off tired relatives or run errands. Volunteers also co-ordinate a team that stays in touch with relatives by telephone for a year after a patient dies.

De Groot spends at least an hour with new patients, determining how they are coping with the prospect of imminent death. She has them set goals for themselves—figure out what they want to do during their last days. "For most people it is overwhelming," she says. "You need to help them find ways to overcome the emotional impact." Yet her patients touch her, too, often in profound ways. "You learn from them and you are inspired by them," she says. She recalls a couple in their mid-60s who died within 24 hours of each other of cancer. Just before the wife took her last breath, the husband—succumbing to the last stages of a brain tumor and seemingly in a coma—reached over and took her hand. "That one act spoke volumes about the relationship between those two people," says De Groot. "It transformed their 30-year-old daughter's understanding of the experience of death."

Thinking of a week when she visited three patients who were born the same year she was, De Groot concedes: "Sometimes my work hits pretty close to home." She sometimes has to talk firmly to patients, such as a man in his mid-40s who tried twice to commit suicide. "Your nine-year-old son is watching how you manage your death," she reminded him. "He will always remember how you died." That, De Groot says, snapped the man out of his despair and allowed him to seize his last moments of life.

Up to a third of patients will experience deep melancholy, De Groot says, a problem that is usually alleviated with antidepressants. "Often people who are considering suicide are those who feel overwhelmed by their pain or symptoms or feel abandoned and despairing." One of her jobs is to recognize a patient's inclination to become depressed and step in with medication if necessary.

De Groot says she cannot condone doctor-assisted suicide but she respects a patient's decision to end his or her life. "As a physician there are two questions to consider," she says. "Do I think patients have a right to choice? Yes. But do I personally feel I have the right to take another's life? No. It's not for me to decide when you'll die." However, she will not try to revive a dying patient who has taken an overdose, nor will she resuscitate a patient who experiences cardiac arrest, unless he or she requested it beforehand. "We shouldn't prolong life at any cost," De Groot says. "For most of our patients, it's medically futile since they are already so close to death."

On Dying with Personhood

Van Rensselaer Potter

Van Rensselaer Potter, who is approximately ninety years old, defines an unacceptable quality of life as mental or physical disability severe enough to require permanent entry into a nursing home. Rather than live this way, he says, he would prefer to die, like the ancient Greek philosopher Socrates, in full possession of his "personhood," which he defines as "the whole spectrum of consciousness." Potter is a retired professor in oncology at the University of Wisconsin, Madison, and is also associated with the McArdle Laboratory for Cancer Research. He frequently writes about global bioethics.

For older adults, dying with personhood is better than living without it in a nursing home at $4800 a month. As noted by Norman Cousins, "Death is not the ultimate tragedy of life. The ultimate tragedy is depersonalization." As I approach the end of my ninth decade of a good life devoted to cancer research and bioethics, I am led to ask about the nature of a good death. Unable to prevent the deaths of my closest colleagues (Harold Rusch, Elizabeth Miller, Charles Heidelberger, Howard Temin, and Helen Iverson), who suffered bad deaths as a result of cancer, I am led to wonder about the possibility that people might have more choice in their final days. We need to call on all the personhood we can muster as we hope to manage death in the context of "dying well." The concept of dying with personhood might very well be called Socratic Death.

In the remarkable and authoritative book *Death, Dying and the Biological Revolution: Our Last Quest for Responsibility*, Robert Veatch concludes with a chapter on "Natural Death and Public Policy." His purpose was "to affirm that deciding in individual cases that the struggle against death need not continue is not incompatible with a more general social commitment to a public policy that sees at least some deaths as evil, that promotes research to overcome them." But throughout the book and, indeed, in all the contemporary discussions known to me, the idea that "the struggle against death need not continue" is in the context of patients who are terminally ill and/or beyond help from medical technology. Here we may ask what about the individual who is in full possession of personhood, not terminally ill as presently defined, but on the threshold of the frailties of advanced old age—total incontinence, loss of mobility, loss of personhood—all subject to what amounts to a kind of terminal illness: confinement in a nursing home. This is the person who wishes to die retaining personhood to the end: what I shall call "Socratic Death."

The Time to Die

Although Socrates had taken the position that "Man is a prisoner who has no right to open the door of his prison and run away. . . . A man should wait, and not take his own life until God summons him," he did in fact end his own life by drinking poison when he had no other choice. In 399 BC, at the command of the Athenian tyranny, he was condemned to death by poison after being accused of corrupting the youth of Athens with his philosophy. But he maintained his personhood to the end, talking with his friends during his last hours before finally drinking a cup of hemlock. Then he lay down on his couch and died in peace, or so we are told. And he was apparently ready to die: According to Veatch, Socrates was said to remark that "When man has reached my age, he ought not to be repining at the approach of death." (Socrates had reached the age of 70, according to estimates of his time of birth.)

For Socrates, the choice of "the time to die" was made for him. For others who wish to die with personhood, the problem is a little more complicated, but a clear-cut sign can be imagined. For me, if not already cut down by events beyond my control, the time will have arrived when my family, personal physician, and social worker agree that there is no other choice than to place me in a nursing home. That is the day for me to die with personhood.

Appropriate medical organizations need to examine the philosophy of a social policy that results in the expenditure of huge sums of money for long-term care of older adults in nursing homes, while 43.4 million people, including children, are without medical insurance according to an estimate by the U.S. Census Bureau. The policy is based on the theory that death is evil and that it should be postponed for as long as possible under conditions frequently made acceptable by the administration of mood-altering drugs such as Prozac or Zoloft [antidepressants]. More information is needed, but the theory seems to rest on false assumptions that mislead both the residents and their caretakers. Death is not evil in an older person when it is chosen voluntarily and for good reason, especially when the person does not wish to live in an unacceptable state of helplessness and at great expense. A *New York Times* editorial (1 January 1999) noted: "Medicaid is currently the major financing source for custodial care but it is available only to people with extremely low incomes, others have to deplete nearly all of their assets before qualifying for

Medicaid. But because nursing home costs are so high, more than half of the people entering nursing homes become so impoverished that they qualify for Medicaid after less than a year." The editorial favors putting the long-term care problem on the nation's political agenda hoping that it might become "a starting point for increased federal involvement." Here is a social policy determined by the theory that death is evil and that it should be delayed as long as possible in all older persons in nursing homes. This is nonsense. We don't know how many older persons would choose to die if given the option, and we don't know how many have lost their personhood before admission to nursing homes or how many lose it during subsequent years. In the case of long-term care it seems unlikely that there are any ongoing social studies that would provide information as to how many residents no longer have "personhood," or how long they have been in that state; considerations on behalf of human dignity preclude thorough studies on the matter. Therefore, it ought to be the responsibility of the attending physician for those residents of nursing homes to keep meaningful records which would give some indication as to whether or not personhood had been diminished or lost. Any indication of the preferences of such persons while they could reflect on their lives is central to guiding future decisions about Socratic Death.

When Personhood Is Threatened

I am in communication with a physician who is a geriatrician [specialist in treating old people] with many years of experience in long-term care and who believes that many residents have lost what we can recognize as an image of personhood. Depending on the selection of criteria of the nursing home, the numbers of residents who have lost their personhood might vary from 15 to 90 percent. This is a tragic situation to which public policy has not been sensitively responsive. Those who hold to the belief that even those individuals without personhood should be preserved from death at all extremes of medical intervention have not faced the full burden of this personhood-less condition.

> To be allowed to die comfortably when personhood is threatened or voided is a dignified grace. The decision should be voluntary, and the case of those unable to make it leaves society in the depths of a problem that has no easy solution.

Here we have a profound issue, the idea that to allow a patient to die comfortably "when personhood is threatened or voided" is to grant the patient the favor of dignity. Granting that the decision should be voluntary "the problem of those unable to make it" leaves society in the depths of a problem so far unresolved. It is this problem that has been taken up by the author of a short note in a winter 1999 issue of this journal. The author is concerned with just one agonizing question:

"Can one ensure a dignified death after dementia sets in?" He proposes the formation of a mutual support society while failing to mention the classic case of Janet Adkins and the existence of the Hemlock Society. Janet Adkins had been diagnosed with Alzheimer's and she resolved to end her life while still able to take action. She contacted Dr. Jack Kevorkian; indeed, she was his first case of assisted suicide.

The founder of the University Alzheimer Center at Case Western Reserve has commented helpfully:

> Dignity—reflecting both personal preferences for life and death and social rules and relationships—seems a central concept. Some like Adkins may decide to end a life with dementia to escape the later ravages of the disease. Others have written living wills asking for euthanasia when the dementia deepens. More community and international discussion is needed to evolve new consciences and consciousness about this important topic—the choices of death with dementia.

At the same time, a new complication has entered "The Dementia Dilemma" in an avalanche of new developments that the author of the *Perspectives* piece may not even be aware of: the emergence of anti-dementia drugs. As noted in an editorial accompanying a discussion of these drugs, in raising questions about the ethics of anti-dementia drugs the authors have "touched the tip of a very important iceberg." Deep within that iceberg lies an equation that no one has explored. The problem, given the limitations of dementia patients, is how to counterbalance the choice for a dignified assisted death against the experimental testing of drugs that are promoted as possible relief from mental incapacity. Add to that the impact of the hope engendered by the drug program on the idea of a dignified death by choice expressed in the early stages of dementia. What would Janet Adkins have done if offered an experimental drug? There is a vast difference between the testing of experimental drugs in mentally competent cancer patients and the testing of drugs in patients with Alzheimer's disease at whatever stage. Here, ethical guidelines are simply inadequate.

Personhood at Dying Time

In all of the foregoing discussion the key issue of the present essay has been overlooked. We need to focus on the role of personhood in the name of dignity at the time of death. Despite the flurry of opinions before and after the June 1997 U.S. Supreme Court decision that we have no constitutional right to physician-assisted suicide, to my knowledge there has been no discussion of the role of personhood at the time of death. Yet the principle of patient autonomy is an ethic that assumes personhood: it requires an examination of what we mean by the word and how it relates to a good death. When dying time arrives, concerned loved ones need to consider the logic of suicide, because the amount of time devoted to suffering prior to death in order to convince spouses and grown children that death is appropriate places too great a burden on the patient and on any attending physician who is called upon for an assisted suicide. Meanwhile, any quick or instant demise by gunshot, razor blade, prescribed medication, or lethal injection before terminal suffering has become an issue is unacceptable to society. A further problem arises when the diagnosis is for a pending loss of personhood through intense suffering or mental degeneration. That is the time when—as in the case of a cancer patient who shot himself and left a note saying "It is not decent for society to make a man do this to himself"—patient autonomy and assisted suicide or personally administered lethal prescription reach the ultimate decision point. The need for mature personhood is called for, not only in the patient but in the family and in the attending physician. Even if the patient is no longer able to make decisions as a result of Alzheimer's disease or other dementia, family and physician would need mature personhood in an area still undefined. The patient with advanced dementia is truly a patient without personhood.

The Concept of Personhood

Personhood is a word that is strictly analogous to a much older word: motherhood. In both cases, the suffix "-hood" creates confusion that needs to be clarified, because of its two-fold meaning: the word can refer to a state, a condition; or it can imply a quality, a characteristic set of features. Thus any woman who has children is in a state of motherhood; if she is a good mother, she exhibits the quality we associate with motherhood, and we can explore the qualities that define a good mother. To say that any woman with children has motherhood defeats the meaning of the word.

As in the case of mother and motherhood, it is wrong to say that since any human being can be called a person, and, if a person, to have personhood. To say that every human being has personhood defeats the meaning. We need to apply the word personhood only to persons having the qualities we associate with the word; we need to explore the spectrum of qualities that can be proposed, to define personhood to our own satisfaction. There have been many articles with attempts to define personhood, although Veatch prefers not to use the term that he considers ambiguous. But we all know personhood when we see it, and we are saddened when we visit a nursing home and sense its loss in some of our friends.

The concept of personhood should be incorporated into the holistic image of human health. Its definition should be the ongoing subject of psycho-social as well as biological investigations that conceptualize personhood and devise methods of study. The concept of person in the strict sense is an eclectic definition of personhood, in which

human individuals possess the whole spectrum of consciousness, reasoning ability, self-motivated activity, self-control, the capacity to
communicate, the presence of self-awareness, and a capacity to exercise autonomy with a sense of moral responsibility that extends
beyond self to community: qualities debated in an extensive literature
not reviewed here. These qualities form the foundation of what we
call personality. Ideally, a fully developed personhood would incorpo-
rate moral responsibility into a sense of compassion, a purpose, and a
reason for existence.

The Rise and Fall of Personhood

The capacity for developing personhood is not fully present in the
fetus or in the newborn. That capacity and that quality grow incrementally during childhood and adolescence. Parents should themselves be mature persons and should foster the development of personhood in their offspring. Parenthood should be seen as a status that
calls for personhood. Present statistics suggest an appalling failure of
parents and of society, locally and worldwide, to protect the health
and to foster the personhood of our children, whose total needs
should be primordial in an ethical society. Medical "bioethics" people
have not given adequate attention to the health and the development
of personhood in growing children and adolescents: from their earli-
est years, children should be taught that death is inevitable for everyone, for every living thing. They need to understand that it is the fact
of death that gives life meaning and that teaches us to cherish life.
Having cherished life we can approach death in later life with honor
and without fear.

The concept of personhood impacts medical science and medical
ethics acutely as individuals reach a peak of personhood, when they
can be real assets to society, and then decline to a terminal stage, at
some point no longer persons in the strict sense. Before this terminal
stage many people will not be self-sufficient and will be physically
handicapped, but they will still be persons in the strict sense. At this
point they should be declared terminally ill. The use of medical technology, feel-good prescriptions, and extended societal resources for
lives no longer sentient, communicating, or responsible, and no
longer motivated for the preservation of life itself seems irrational and
little short of obscene. Yet this is the mode of operation in today's
nursing homes for long-term care. Here we have a perfect example of
what Richard Lamm challenged when he pointed out that "current
medical ethics assume the health care system must do everything
'beneficial' for every patient. This is an unsustainable standard
because it does not recognize the law of diminishing returns. . . . It is
a yardstick that is unsustainable and will bankrupt our children." In
many cases doing the "beneficial" thing may be to respect the idea of
dying with personhood. Current medical ethics has not been alone in

bypassing public policy: following the original concept of bioethics as a bridge to the future, global bioethics emphasized the need to combine medical and environmental bioethics but failed to emphasize that both of these pursuits entail vast sums of money that must be collected and spent in the framework of public policy. Thus as we enter the 21st century and the Third Millennium, bioethics must embrace a global socio-bioethics, in which public policy moves toward global health and environmental needs while emphasizing financial policies that consider the welfare of all the people.

Personhood in Nursing Homes

Since the concept of personhood as "persons in the strict sense" implies a capacity to exercise autonomy, the question arises as to how much choice is available for the person who has reached the dying time. Can anyone choose the time and manner of achieving a good death, of "dying well"? If the choice is not to be made by God, or by physicians, or by physicians "leaving it up to God," then does it not fall to patients who have personhood, or who have declared their choice in the past when they still had choice? May a diabetic refuse to receive insulin? Are there any cases on record? Is the case of the diabetic in a nursing home rationally wishing to die not an issue for our medical ethics people?

The ethical decisions in connection with long-term care in nursing homes or other forms of assisted living become acute as the residents' lives become less and less meaningful through the gradual loss of the various qualities of personhood. To what extent should effort be expended to maintain life on the basis of a once competent and highly respected personhood that is no longer expressed—as perhaps epitomized in the dreaded Alzheimer's disease, in which the logic of suicide may no longer be grasped—when the patient has failed to declare a choice when still competent?

The ethical decisions in connection with long-term care for patients who are no longer in possession of personhood are not merely whether the ethic of "sanctity of life" should override all other considerations: the monetary costs to society and to surviving relatives becomes a public policy issue. We need an accounting of all the money spent on nursing homes. In the case of expensive technology for younger patients in full possession of their personhood, data are available for ESRD (end-stage renal [kidney] disease); for example, in 1996 the estimated total direct monetary cost of treatment in the United States was $14.55 billion. The total costs for the large numbers of heart, lung, and heart-lung transplants are incalculable, but these costs are also outside clinical ethics at present. Again, public policy should be considered, and the cost of long-term care in nursing homes should not be overlooked.

The three most important life occasions for people are birth, parenthood, and death. Born without personhood and with no choice in the matter, we need to develop it and use it to exercise choice in parenthood and in advanced age if and when fate permits some options. For older adults the goal of dying with personhood means dying with dignity preserved, after a good life. For young persons the goal of public policy should be a good life, lived with health and dignity in a bioethical world of mutual service and respect, until permitted to die with personhood in old age. Public policy should respect the idea that dying with personhood may involve dying by means of a legally prescribed substance when dying time arrives, as in the Death With Dignity Act approved for terminally ill patients in the state of Oregon in 1997.

LET'S NOT NORMALIZE SUICIDE

Marjorie Williams

A frequent writer for the *Washington Post* (where she was formerly a staff member) as well as a contributing editor to *Vanity Fair*, Marjorie Williams says that caring for her dying mother persuaded her that the experience of death should not be cut short by assisted suicide. To do so, she believes, creates temptation for dying people and their families to think they can "manage death away." It deprives them of valuable lessons to be learned from the feeling of powerlessness that is part of mortality, she writes.

In its October 1999 vote to overrule Oregon's first-in-the-nation law permitting physician-assisted suicide [by approving the Pain Relief Promotion Act], the Republican House of Representatives showed its usual heavy hand in dealing with delicate social issues. There was major hypocrisy, to say the least, in conservatives' sudden discovery that some issues are too important to be decided at the state level. But it's hard for me to shake an increasing sympathy for the ethical imperative on which the House was acting.

My mother was a great advocate of the dignified exit. As she neared 70, she gathered a collection of books from the Hemlock Society [an organization that advocates physician-assisted suicide], polished her living will and joked about having a friend dispatch her with a pillow if she ever languished in a nursing home. Once, when I sought to probe a little past her jokes and brisk comments, she gave me a look that I saw only half a dozen times in my life with her: unguarded, unvarnished by good manners. "Don't you know?" she asked. "Whenever there's no one your age around, that's all people my age talk about."

But it was her death, from liver failure, that overturned my settled assumptions about assisted suicide. As far as I am able to say, my mother's was an "easy" death. She wasn't in terrible pain. She was at home, in the house she had loved for more than 35 years into a place of comfort and grace; she was surrounded by her three daughters and a group of women friends who tiptoed in each day with small offerings of the spring flowers that bloomed just in time. She had all the comforts and care it is possible to buy, and, in her hospice nurse, the good fortune that has no price. From the time she entered hospice care to the morning of her death was a little under three weeks.

The Value of Bearing the Unbearable

Yet even this short, kind end was excruciating to be a part of. She looked, at the very least, miserably uncomfortable. On the days when she unexpectedly drifted back to us, out of her semi-coma, she seemed to want something nameless, out of our power to deliver or even guess. Her dying seemed, during those weeks, an endless state, a slow, inconsistent progress that made each day open before us with dreary mystery. The nurses would tell us what we might expect, from the clinical (the cooling of the extremities that would signal the slowing of circulation) to the superstitious (pets, one nurse told us, sometimes come to lie down with an owner when death is imminent). The childlike intensity with which we, three women in our forties, watched for these signs—Look! The cat is on the bed! No, Annie brought him up and put him there earlier—told us how painful it was to drift through a crucial passage that was so entirely beyond our control.

Later I found things in that time to value: the privilege of caring well for her, the tenderness of the bond I shared with my sisters. But as we lived it, we felt most clearly our powerlessness. It was so big, that feeling, that I began to wonder if human beings can really be trusted with the suggestion that there are ways to make the process manageable, to combat the losses of autonomy and control that are the essence of death. You bear the unbearable, in the orbit of a loved one's death, because you have to. If we come to believe that we and our families can sometimes be spared that, how many of us will be willing to endure it at all, under any circumstances?

This concern is somewhat borne out by the Oregon Health Division's report on the first year after passage of the state's suicide act, issued in February 1999. Of the 21 persons who secured lethal prescriptions from their doctors in 1998, 15 of whom went through with their suicides, only one cited the fear of intractable pain. More than anything, these patients cited concerns about "autonomy and personal control." Advocates of Oregon's system point out that it includes an elaborate series of safety mechanisms, of waiting periods and second opinions and witnesses not related to the dying person, to ensure against family pressure and medical cost-cutting and all the other obviously sinister temptations that are said to lurk at the bottom of the slippery slope.

But I wonder now if it is that very structure—the sensible, humane, normalizing particulars by which suicide is enshrined in social policy—that constitutes the threat, because it offers such reassuring authority to anyone who might be tempted to manage death away.

In other words, to us all. I can easily imagine circumstances far worse than my mother's. I wouldn't dream of judging anyone—physician, patient or family—who privately chose to end or help end the unendurable. But officially, publicly, in the open realm where our norms develop, I hope we continue to honor the assumption that death is the one matter that is out of our hands.

How People Feel About End-of-Life Issues

John M. Benson

In this selection, John M. Benson, deputy director of the Harvard Opinion Research Program at the Harvard School of Public Health, summarizes the results of opinion polls made in the United States in the 1970s, 1980s, and 1990s. He describes changes in citizens' feelings about such end-of-life issues as forgoing life-sustaining treatment, administration of pain medication in doses that may hasten death (the "double effect"), voluntary active euthanasia, and physician-assisted suicide. Benson claims that, on the whole, people have become more accepting of consensual practices that result in the death of terminally ill patients.

During the late 1990s and early 2000s, issues at the end of human life have become increasingly prominent in the media and in the political arena. Books by Derek Humphry, Marilyn Webb, and Sherwin B. Nuland brought end-of-life issues to a broad reading public. Euthanasia came into American homes on the evening of November 22, 1998, when the popular television news magazine *60 Minutes* broadcast a story containing excerpts from a video of Dr. Jack Kevorkian administering lethal medication to a 52-year-old man with Lou Gehrig's Disease (ALS, or amyotrophic lateral sclerosis).

In 1997, the U.S. Supreme Court (in *Vacco v. Quill*, 117 S. Ct. 2293, and *Washington v. Glucksberg*, 117 S. Ct. 2258) overturned two lower court rulings that had found a constitutional right to die. In the 1990s, four states voted on ballot initiatives to legalize physician-assisted suicide, and one such initiative was passed by voters in Oregon in 1994.

The right-to-life movement, which played an important role in end-of-life debates as far back as the Nancy Cruzan case in the late 1980s, has begun to focus even more of its attention on the end of life. Antiabortion forces have been in the forefront of opposition to physician-assisted suicide referenda and are the main impetus for "lethal dose" legislation that would use drug-control laws to make it illegal for a doctor to prescribe enough painkillers to help a patient

From "The Polls—Trends End-of-Life Issues," by John M. Benson, *Public Opinion Quarterly*, Summer 1999. Copyright © 1999 The University of Chicago Press. Used with permission of the University of Chicago Press (on behalf of the American Association for Public Opinion Research).

commit suicide. In addition, they have been pursuing laws that would limit the ability of relatives to halt the artificial feeding or life support of patients who cannot make such decisions themselves.

With the graying of the Baby Boom generation, end-of-life issues are likely to remain on the public stage for many years to come. In the review that follows, we look at trends in public attitudes about forgoing life-sustaining treatment, "double effect," voluntary active euthanasia (VAE), and physician-assisted suicide (PAS).

Forgoing Life-Sustaining Treatment

Major organizations of health care professionals make careful distinctions when discussing ethics in end-of-life care. The American Medical Association's Council on Ethical and Judicial Affairs (AMA-CEJA) endorses the duty of physicians to respect the wishes of competent patients to forgo life-sustaining treatment, as well as the practice of providing effective pain treatment even though it might hasten death. The council does not, however, endorse assisted suicide or active euthanasia. Judging from the data presented here, the public does not make precisely the same distinctions.

Trend data on the question of withholding or withdrawing (forgoing) life-sustaining treatment are incomplete, with no trend carrying forward later than 1991, but the direction is clear. Each of five trend questions posits a situation where the patient is hopelessly or terminally ill or irreversibly comatose, and where the patient or family expresses a desire not to have or continue treatment. In the last year of each of the five trends, at least three-fourths of American adults favored withholding or withdrawing treatment in the scenario described.

Two of the trends indicate a shift in public opinion during the 1970s and early 1980s toward greater support for withdrawing or withholding treatment. The level of support has remained about steady from 1985 on.

In addition, a trend using a more generally phrased question indicates growing support between 1982 and 1991 for allowing doctors to honor the written instructions of their patients, even if it means allowing them to die. This question may have been seen by various respondents as dealing with any or all of the end-of-life situations discussed in this article.

Living wills are the best-known form of written instruction in cases where a patient is unconscious and suffering from a terminal illness. The enactment in 1991 of the Patient Self-Determination Act (PSDA) was expected by its proponents to increase greatly the proportion of Americans who filled out living wills and health care proxies. Unfortunately, no consistently worded trend measures the prevalence of such documents, although it appears from fragmentary evidence that living wills are slightly more common today than they were a decade ago.

"Double Effect" Administration of Pain Medication

The AMA-CEJA report considers it ethical for a physician to provide pain treatment even though it may foreseeably hasten death. This practice is sometimes called "the doctrine of double effect."

The two available trends measuring public attitudes about double effect are incomplete, beginning and ending in the 1980s. The data show no change in attitudes between 1982 and 1987, with about three-fourths of the public supporting such a practice.

Voluntary Active Euthanasia

Voluntary active euthanasia (VAE) differs from "double effect" in that, on the request of the patient, the physician administers medication or treatment the intent of which is to end the patient's life. This practice is not condoned in the AMA-CEJA report. The act performed by Dr. Kevorkian in the *60 Minutes* segment is actually VAE. The fact that VAE is sometimes called active PAS leads to considerable confusion about the level of public support.

On the issue of VAE, we have the longest and most complete trends. Each question describes a patient who is dying, terminally or hopelessly ill, or has a disease that cannot be cured, and who makes the request or demand of the physician. About two-thirds of Americans favor VAE in the most recent askings of our trend questions.

The trend data show a considerable rise in public support for VAE from the immediate post–World War II years to the 1970s. Four hypotheses may help explain this growth in support for VAE. First, the low level of support for VAE in 1947 and 1950 may reflect recent memory and fear of practices used by the Nazis in less voluntary settings. A second hypothesis, which may help explain changes in public opinion about both forgoing treatment and VAE during the late 1970s, is that the celebrated case of Karen Ann Quinlan in 1975–1976 helped crystallize the nation's consciousness on end-of-life matters. A third hypothesis is that Americans have increasingly adopted what might be called a secular humanistic view of compassion. Related to this is a fourth hypothesis that these trends represent an increasing desire by Americans for legislation that would permit more personal control over the quality of life and death when they are terminally ill.

Three of the trend questions describe the patient as having "a disease that cannot be cured," rather than a terminal illness. Incurable diseases that are not terminal might include degenerative diseases like ALS. While this difference in question wording is medically and perhaps ethically important, it does not seem to affect the public's response.

A rather abbreviated trend measuring public attitudes about the Oregon physician-assisted suicide law is worded in a way that characterizes it as VAE. This trend shows support at about the same level as in other VAE questions.

Physician-Assisted Suicide

Physician-assisted suicide (PAS) differs from VAE in that the person takes his or her own life, assisted by the physician, who would typically give the patient a prescription for a lethal drug. PAS is not condoned in the AMA-CEJA report.

The trend data do not tell us very much about long-term changes in attitudes about PAS, since none of the available trends go back before 1990. We see the expected stability in support during the course of the 1990s. The public shows considerably less support for PAS than for VAE. Through all the variations in question wording, between 45 percent and 59 percent support PAS.

The lower level of public support for PAS than for VAE provides an interesting insight into some of the forces that undergird public opinion on end-of-life issues. One might have expected the public to have a more favorable view of a practice where the patient controls the timing and final administration of the life-ending act and the physician merely provides the means. But other considerations, such as an instinctive aversion to and religious proscriptions against suicide or fear that the suffering patient might act too rashly, evidently affect the responses of many Americans. Such a discussion lies outside the bounds of a trends article.

In two cross-national studies conducted in 1981 and 1990, more Americans express negative judgments about suicide than about euthanasia. During the trend's decade, the proportion who saw euthanasia as "never" justified dropped from 47 percent to 36 percent, although few felt the practice was "always" justified.

Americans are not entirely averse to suicide in cases of terminal illness. Currently six in ten Americans believe that a person has a right to end his or her own life if that person has an incurable disease. As we have seen in several other trends, public support for a right to commit suicide in cases of terminal illness has risen considerably since the late 1970s.

About one-third (32 percent) of adults, in both 1991 and 1998, said that if they were seriously ill with a terminal disease, they would consider suicide. Relatively few Americans, however, would be willing to help a terminally ill relative or close friend commit suicide to end his or her suffering.

Given how often Dr. Kevorkian has been in the news over the past several years, we might have expected more trend data about his actions. The two trends we have show public attitudes split. Public disapproval of Dr. Kevorkian's actions increased between 1993 and 1998.

Conclusions

This review of trends in public opinion about end-of-life issues highlights some limitations in the available data. Aside from the dearth of long-term trends, some important aspects of the problem have not been measured consistently over time. For instance, the existing questions focus on cases of terminal or hopeless diseases, usually stating or implying that the patients and their families give unequivocal expression to their wishes. In the real world, circumstances are often more complex.

In addition, none of the trend questions present arguments that might discourage support for PAS or VAE, such as the argument that legalization creates a slippery slope to less voluntary practices. The New York State Task Force on Life and the Law (1997) lists 10 risks associated with legalization of PAS, including a sense of obligation to die, vulnerability of socially marginalized groups, devaluation of the lives of the disabled, and increasing financial incentives to limit care.

Pain management, an important issue in end-of-life situations, has received little attention in the available polling. In spite of the right-to-life movement's concerns about end-of-life decisions, no consistently worded trend measures whether or not Americans consider VAE and PAS to be murder.

Taken as a whole, the trend data show a growth of support for various consensual practices that result in the death of terminally ill patients. Most of that change occurred by the early 1980s, and public opinion has been rather stable since then. The most current data also show that the public's views are not entirely in line with the medical establishment's view of ethical physician behavior. Finally, the public seems able to differentiate broadly among various end-of-life situations and among possible life-takers.

CHAPTER 2

PHYSICIANS AND ASSISTED DEATH

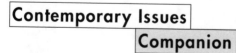

Assisting a Patient's Suicide Violates Medical Ethics

Nelson Lund

Nelson Lund, a professor of law at George Mason University in Arlington, Virginia, believes that legally permitting physicians to assist in a patient's suicide, even if the patient is terminally ill, violates the trusting relationship that should exist between doctor and patient. That relationship, he says, was defined by the ancient Greek Hippocratic Oath, a classic statement of medical ethics. When taking that oath, Lund claims, physicians promise never to give or recommend a deadly drug. Lund has been coeditor of several volumes of the *Supreme Court Economic Review*.

In January 1997 the Supreme Court heard oral arguments in two cases that could generate a constitutional right to physician-assisted suicide. Several justices seemed skeptical about the wisdom of creating such a right, and we all should hope that the court will resist the temptation to authorize doctors to kill their patients. Otherwise, we soon will witness a new and barbaric culture of euthanasia and bureaucratized death.

Why shouldn't patients be free to have their doctors help in using lethal drugs to end their suffering? The answer lies in the special nature of the doctor-patient relationship. Anyone who has been seriously ill knows something about the tremendous power that physicians exert over their patients. Physicians have a virtual monopoly over the information patients use to make decisions about their own treatment, and they are experts at presenting the options in a way that almost guarantees which choice the patient will make. This is not necessarily inappropriate. We hire doctors, after all, because they know more than we do about treating our illnesses. But it does require us to assume that doctors have our interests at heart when they make their recommendations.

For thousands of years, the medical profession has recognized that patients will not place the necessary trust in doctors who behave like ordinary tradesmen. With the Hippocratic oath, every doctor promises neither to give a deadly drug to anybody if asked for it nor to make a suggestion to this effect. The oath is an offer to make a bargain with patients: "In return for your placing more trust in us than you do in ordinary tradesmen, we promise to behave in a less self-interested manner than other tradesmen." This is a good bargain for both parties: Physicians get more business because sick people will be less inclined to practice home remedies, and patients get better medical care when they are treated by experts.

The bargain implicit in the Hippocratic oath, however, is not self-enforcing. Traditionally, state legislatures have promoted the medical profession's monopoly by restricting unauthorized medical practice and by giving physicians exclusive control over powerful drugs. In return, state laws have required physicians to abide by key tenets of the Hippocratic oath, including the ban on assisted suicide and euthanasia.

If the federal courts strike down the laws against assisted suicide, they will unleash legions of Jack Kevorkians, and worse. First some doctors will be manipulating seriously ill patients into agreeing to assisted suicide, and others will begin practicing euthanasia when they are confident the patient would agree to commit suicide if he or she could. Second, patients rightly will become much more distrustful of their doctors' advice, and this distrust will make it much more difficult to give appropriate care.

If these predictions seem alarmist, consider the Dutch experience. After the taboo against assisted suicide was relaxed in the Netherlands beginning in 1984, physicians quickly went straight down the slippery slope. A privately financed survey in 1989 showed that 40 percent of Dutch physicians had performed euthanasia without patients' consent. Other surveys have produced similar results. And what reasons did physicians give for these homicides? Intractable pain was mentioned in less than a third of the cases. More commonly physicians mentioned "low quality of life, the relatives, inability to cope and no prospect for improvement."

Intractable pain, especially among the terminally ill, is a genuine problem, but only because the American medical profession has been scandalously negligent in dealing with it. Nor has an obsessive fixation with the dangers of drug addiction helped matters. But the way to deal with this problem is by encouraging the profession to take pain relief much more seriously than it now does. Killing the patient is cheaper, and it may be appealing to overburdened relatives and profit-seeking managed-care companies, but it is not the practice of medicine.

Replacing the clear ban against doctors killing their patients with detailed government regulations inevitably would increase intrusiveness into the doctor-patient relationship. It would not prevent abuses by doctors and their bureaucratic overseers, since it is relatively easy for doctors to kill their patients without getting caught. That is exactly why the clear professional ethic forbidding such conduct should be reinforced rather than undermined.

ASSISTING A PATIENT'S SUICIDE CAN BE ETHICAL

Peter Reagan

Peter Reagan is a physician in Oregon, the only state in the United States in which it is legal for physicians to help terminally ill patients commit suicide. In this selection, Reagan describes his involvement in the assisted death of Helen, a woman in her eighties who was dying of breast cancer. He tells how he, Helen, and her two adult children fulfilled the requirements of Oregon's Death with Dignity law. Finally, he explains why he feels that assisting in Helen's death, far from being a violation of medical ethics, was an honor and a profoundly transforming experience.

She pointed to her left cheek and said, "You can kiss me now. Right here". Taken by surprise, and extremely moved, I kissed her lightly and sat back. She smiled and looked up brightly. Afterwards she asked me for some brandy. Beth had diluted it fifty-fifty with a soft drink. She wasn't used to drinking much alcohol, and she choked on it just a little as it went down. Beth offered her a mint, but she waved it away and said she was sleepy. Douglas held her right hand and arm, as I held her left. Beth massaged her feet. Her breathing was slow, even, and relaxed. About a minute later I asked her how she was doing and she mumbled, "Tired". We took two of the pillows from behind her head so she could sit back more easily, and Helen fell into a deep sleep.

The three of us sat around her bed talking quietly about the emotional struggle we'd each been through. 3 weeks earlier, I had received a phone call from a retired colleague about a patient who wanted help ending her life under the Oregon Death With Dignity Law, which went into effect in October 1997. Her previous physicians had not been prepared to offer a life-ending prescription. Could I see her soon?

5 days later she was sitting in a wheelchair in an examination room with her son Douglas and her daughter Beth. She was elderly, frail, and hooked to oxygen, but completely astute, with a delightful twinkle; I liked her immediately. She and her family carefully detailed her history of breast cancer, her years since her first mastectomy, the recurrence on the other side, the metastases, and the downhill course.

The second tumour had developed when she was 82; she had refused all treatment for it after the lumpectomy. Her husband had suffered a lingering death a decade earlier; she was opting for life while it was good and then a clean exit.

Meeting the Law's Requirements

I discussed the requirements of the law with her. When I got to the part about a written request, she handed me a notarised statement signed by Douglas and a neighbour. I looked into her eyes and shivered as I contemplated the enormity of what I was facing. I took a deep breath and we started discussing her attempts to get help with dying. She had asked her original physician, but he was about to relocate his practice and didn't want to be involved. He had recommended hospice care and had referred her to a second primary physician who, he thought, might have been open to aid in dying. The second physician had seen her twice, ordered a chest radiograph, and also encouraged hospice care. He agreed that she had a short life-expectancy but recorded in her notes that she was probably depressed. Helen and her family felt he was not ready to provide assistance and was buying time. She said, "He made me wait 24 days, and he never intended to help me. I think he still expected me to come back to him. He should have told me at the beginning".

I sympathised with her reluctant previous physicians, but I was quite impressed by this earnest family and their determined mother. I sensed that I was missing something. Helen was very ill and obviously getting worse, but she was managing in a wheelchair, she had a great family, and she had a wonderful sense of humour. Why was she in such a hurry to die? I told her that, although I was supportive of her right and desire to seek help, I didn't want her to die, and hoped she might choose to wait.

The next day I was talking on the phone to Douglas and Beth. Helen needed a psychiatric consultation since her previous physician had written that she was depressed, and I arranged an appointment later in the week. She also needed a second opinion from a specialist about her life-expectancy. Helen complained to her children about how cumbersome the new law was, and we talked about how the law wasn't supposed to make it easy. I also asked for permission to discuss the case with the carers at Helen's hospice. The family felt supported by the carers, with whom they had discussed Helen's request. Although the hospice's policy did not support any use of the Death with Dignity Law, the nurses were eager to provide as much comfort as possible to the family and also to me.

The psychiatrist called me 2 days later. During a home visit lasting 90 minutes or so, he had painstakingly evaluated Helen's competence and her mood, and concluded that she showed no signs of depression. My own impression confirmed, I had to accept that this really was going to happen. Of course I could choose not to participate. The thought of Helen dying so soon was almost too much to bear, and only slightly less difficult was the knowledge that many very reasonable people would consider aiding in her death a crime. On the other hand, I found even worse the thought of disappointing this family. If I backed out, they'd feel about me the way they had about their previous doctor, that I had strung them along, and in a way, insulted them.

In a Hurry to Die?

A week after the first visit, Helen, Douglas, and Beth were back in my office. Helen was chipper and witty, but obviously failing. She liked the oxygen she had received from the hospice, but knew her breathing continued to worsen. We talked about how things had gone so far. She reported that ever since she had known I was receptive to her request, her life had become more relaxed and she could enjoy her family more.

Helen again complained about waiting so long, so I pressed her to explain her haste. She said she was worried she might lose her mental faculties, and she had some anxiety that something might happen to change the law itself. But the most important thing to Helen was that each day was worse than the day before, and she expected no further value from her life. She didn't see the point in further personal indignities, or in burdening her friends and family with care, because in her mind her life was already over.

She looked at me and profusely thanked me, partly for my support, and partly for my understanding. She said that I had brought joy back into her life. I was embarrassed and tried to acknowledge her gratitude for such a complex bittersweet role. We arranged a house-call on Sunday. 2 days later she had her evaluation by the specialist, who called with a report confirming my own observations, equally shaken by her eagerness to die.

My wife discovered a passage in an article by Pieter Admiraal about euthanasia in the Netherlands that seemed to epitomise Helen's feelings. He described a group of patients who lose the ability to do the things that enable them to recognise themselves. From acceptance of their fate they move to a state of complete detachment from life and therefore have no reason to continue bothering with it. They long impatiently for death.

Elizabeth Kubler-Ross, Ram Dass, Stephen Levine, and others have emphasised that the experience of dying with cancer offers an opportunity for spiritual growth and completing unfinished emotional work. I support this concept, but Helen was not interested. She wanted to be conscious of the moment of leaving the world, and was unaware of unfinished business. She would know when to say good-bye, and that all the details were taken care of.

Sunday morning came. I was at Helen's house at 11 am. I wanted to get a feel for where she lived and more about who she was. Douglas and Beth were there, and I met a granddaughter as well. Helen described her childhood in Europe and a relative's death in a concentration camp during World War II. She mentioned her own husband and how difficult his lingering death had been. I wanted to discuss how they felt about my being there when she took the medication. I explained my misgivings about how she might feel pressure. She said she really wanted me to be there because I would be her anchor. A daunting role.

She wondered whether to take the medication sitting in a chair or lying down, and fretted a little about taking the whole dose in less than a minute. But I reassured her that a minute could be a very long time. In fact, I was savouring my minutes with her. In a couple of days, life was going to change for all of us. As I got ready to leave, she looked up at me and grinned, "When you do this thing, you will be able to sleep well at night, because you will know what you did was right". I thanked her and then turned away with my tangle of emotions.

That afternoon, I was sitting at my kitchen table with my file folder of her materials. I wrote and signed prescriptions for two drugs to prevent nausea, ondansetron and metoclopramide, after considering how to customise the dose. Then I wrote the prescription for the 90 secobarbital [a powerful narcotic that can cause death]. I hesitated at the signature and stared out the window. I faced a stunning spring sky full of fluffy cumulus clouds, crisp and full of promise. I tried to imagine deciding to die. I couldn't succeed in putting myself in Helen's place. Whenever I tried, I experienced a sadness much more profound than what I saw in her.

A Peaceful End

I slept badly. I dragged myself out of bed and onto my bicycle to take the prescriptions to her house. The cold morning air felt good on my face. I came in the door and we discussed when I'd be able to come back in the evening. Then, with Helen, I went over the prescribed checklist for the Death with Dignity Law. She had not a moment's hesitation. "Thank you so much, doctor." Off to work . . . The day was full of people with the usual ailments. Overshadowed by Helen's imminent death, life's little vicissitudes didn't look all that earth shattering.

I arrived at 7 pm, and we spent some time together. I couldn't take my eyes off Helen, as she happily reminisced about the old times. After about 5 minutes, Beth went into the kitchen. Helen stopped mid-sentence and said "Shouldn't I take the medicine now?" I pointed out that it wasn't quite ready. She smiled and went back into another little family story. Beth appeared from the kitchen with a cup half full of creamy red liquid. I suggested the family take some time to say their goodbyes, but they said they had already done that. So I took a moment to say how moved and touched I was to have been privileged to care for her. She looked back at me and thanked me, and offered me a cheek. Then she requested the cup.

There was no pause. She drank the entire dose in less than 20 seconds. She looked up, pretty pleased with herself, and asked for the brandy. Then she put her head back and went to sleep within a few minutes. Her breathing got deeper, and she became totally unresponsive. I moved behind her head to help straighten the pillows and checked a carotid pulse, which became thready after 15 minutes.

We three talked about the grandson who was having a birthday, an upcoming wedding, the misgivings of some other family members, and the plans for a service. Helen became pale, and then started agonal respiration [the type of breathing that occurs near death]. This continued for about 10 minutes after we lost her pulse. About half an hour after she had drunk the bitter liquid, all motion ceased. Still we sat, into the night. It was a reflective hour, a gentle, calm time. I really appreciated the chance to join in their awe of the event. I left at about 9 pm.

A Transforming Experience

Experience in the Netherlands, where assisted suicide and euthanasia usually are not prosecuted, suggests that doctors are profoundly affected by an act of physician-assisted suicide. Gerrit Kimsma, a Dutch family physician and medical ethicist, writes with colleagues that some professionals become dysfunctional and may require a lot of time to recover.

There was something a little shocking about Helen's sudden intentional transition from cheerful alertness to death. In a way, her death represented a personal triumph, and the last emotion she communicated to us was the pride of its accomplishment. Our involvement meant that we could share that satisfaction, an unusual experience at a death bed. As Helen's doctor during her last days, I developed an emotional bond with her and her family in the many hours of forthright conversation I had with them. This depth of relationship allowed me to see for myself how intensely she wanted to die. I remain profoundly transformed by her reality.

2 weeks after Helen's death I was at a party, talking with a woman who had been treated for breast cancer during the previous year. As she described her feelings about the illness, the changes in her priorities, the appreciation for the small things in life, and her desire to work less and contemplate more, I began to note that I was similarly affected. It dawned on me that I had experienced the last few days of Helen's life almost as if I were dying too.

A few weeks later I had a chance to meet with Helen's family again. They seemed very much at peace with her death and were getting on well with their own lives. At a subsequent meeting, Helen's previous physician sought me out and thanked me for taking over her care.

The story I have told is mine only and does not do justice to the experience of Helen and her family. I am honoured to have been chosen to work with them. Her death exemplified the elements of determination, courage, pride, compassion, honesty, family devotion, and good humour that embody the best in people. She will be missed.

EVALUATING REQUESTS FOR ASSISTED SUICIDE

E. Emanuel, K. Hedberg, and T. Quill

E. Emanuel is the director of the Department of Clinical Bioethics at the Warren G. Magnuson Clinical Center at the National Institutes of Health in Bethesda, Maryland. K. Hedberg works for the Oregon Health Division as a medical epidemiologist and is on a state-sponsored panel that evaluated the effects of Oregon's Death with Dignity Act. T. Quill is a professor of medicine, psychiatry, and medical humanities at the University of Rochester School of Medicine in New York and a prominent supporter of physician-assisted suicide as an option for terminally ill people. Whether or not a physician is legally permitted or willing to help a terminally ill patient die, these authors point out, the first task of the doctor who receives such a request should be to find out what needs or fears lie behind it. Once physicians know what is troubling their patients, the authors write, they may discover alternatives to suicide. The authors suggest questions for physicians to ask patients who request suicide and ways of meeting these dying patients' needs.

A long-suffering, incurably ill patient asks for help in dying. How should you [the patient's physician] respond? What legal and ethical options exist? What can you do if they fail?

A physician who receives an inquiry from a patient about help in committing suicide is professionally obligated to fully discuss the request with the patient. Formulating a response to a request for physician-assisted suicide is difficult given the extreme desperation and suffering of the patient and the legal and ethical pitfalls involved. Evaluating the request and learning creative methods for handling problematic end-of-life issues may diminish the desire for physician-assisted suicide and can spare physicians significant personal and professional anguish.

When a patient requests physician-assisted suicide, the American Medical Association (AMA) says that the physician's initial response must be to explore the meaning behind the question, regardless of

E. Emanuel, K. Hedberg, and T. Quill, "The Complexities of Assisted Suicide," *Patient Care*, vol. 34, pp. 65–86 (2000). Copyright © 2000 Medical Economics Company. Used with permission.

willingness to participate. Unlike suicidal patients who view death as a form of destruction, terminally ill patients often see death as a form of self-preservation. Disease can ravage the mind and body, rendering a person unrecognizable to him- or herself and to loved ones. Patients may feel that the longer they live with terminal illness, the more they will lose themselves to disease. A request for physician-assisted suicide is not necessarily irrational. Nevertheless, it is never to be taken at face value.

When a patient pleads, "Doctor, please put me out of my misery" resist avoiding the topic or giving an immediate Yes or No answer. Instead, let the request serve as a springboard for discussing end-of-life concerns and options. Willingness to enter into such a conversation constitutes nonabandonment in action and demonstrates that the physician will be neither idle nor apathetic. Get to the heart of the patient's fears by asking

- What kinds of deaths have you experienced in your family?
- Was the process of dying a traumatic experience that you do not want to imitate?
- What is your worst-case scenario?
- What makes you want help with suicide?
- How long have you thought about it?

Determine which aspects of suffering are currently making the patient's life intolerable by asking in your own words

- What symptoms are you experiencing?
- Are you in pain?
- Are you having problems with your family?
- Are you involved in a spiritual crisis?
- Are you depressed?

Based on the answers to these questions, physicians often are able to determine the reason behind a request for physician-assisted suicide. Further discussion may allay the patient's fears about the future, while palliative therapies may resolve any psychological, spiritual, or physical problems prompting the request. Follow up with a reevaluation.

People do not always request physician-assisted suicide directly. Fleeting wishes for a hastened death can be cloaked in phrases such as "I wish it were all over" or "I can't take this anymore." Probe deeper when a patient makes such a remark, and clarify the request: "Are you saying that you want to end your life? What were you hoping I could do to help you?" Or, if covert suicidal thoughts are suspected, the physician could encourage the patient to freely discuss any end-of-life matter, ranging from practical medication questions to existential meaning-of-life concerns.

Why Does the Patient Want to Die?

A number of underlying reasons for a request for help in dying is possible. Loss of control, fear of abandonment or burdening others, financial hardship, physical and psychological symptoms, and personal beliefs are all potential causes of suffering. A recent Canadian study examining the attitudes of terminally ill patients with advanced cancer showed that theoretically, 64% of the 70 participants considered both euthanasia and physician-assisted suicide acceptable practices that should be legalized. Pain and the individual's right to control the manner of death were the top two reasons these participants favored legalization. Of the 12% who reported they would presently request a hastened death if it were legal, only one cited pain as a contributing factor.

Physical pain: A 1990 survey showed that 5% to 35% of patients who were enrolled in hospice programs described their pain as "severe" in the last week of life. Yet recent US and Dutch studies show that physical pain alone is not the most prominent reason dying patients request a hastened death. In the Netherlands, a study of 187 patients showed pain to be a motivating factor in only 10 cases. A study conducted in 1996 was the first to show that pain is not associated with interest in physician-assisted suicide. According to the study, patients experiencing pain were less likely to view physician-assisted suicide as an acceptable measure than were patients suffering from depression and psychological distress. Aggressive palliative medication can usually control physical pain.

Loss of autonomy and dignity: After physician-assisted suicide was legalized in Oregon in 1997, personnel with the Oregon Health Division wanted to assess whether patients were requesting assistance because they were in pain, lacked access to hospice care, did not have medical insurance, or for other reasons. Their studies of the first 2 years of legalization found that the need to control the manner and timing of death was the factor that best defined the majority of patients who requested assistance. Patients were concerned about waning autonomy, losing control of bodily functions, and the logistics of dying. A study showed that 57% of Dutch patients cited loss of dignity as the primary reason for requesting physician-assisted suicide.

Fear of becoming a burden: Many patients who request physician-assisted suicide believe they are a burden on family members, particularly on those serving as caregivers. This is a real and serious issue, particularly in a society that values autonomy as much as America's does. Through discussion, patients who fear emotionally and financially burdening their loved ones may realize that physician-assisted suicide could create an additional burden. Family members and close friends are left to deal with the aftermath of death. Feeling responsible for the patient's death can complicate the grieving process significantly. Hospice, visiting nurse services, and home care personnel can educate patients and families about the alternatives.

Depression: Screening patients for symptoms of depression is essential, as this condition is directly linked to interest in physician-assisted suicide. A request for help in committing suicide is not necessarily a sign of psychopathology or an example of "how anyone would feel" given the situation. Each patient is unique and has different reasons for requesting assistance. When a caring and knowledgeable physician confronts a patient's fears, the desire for help with dying may lessen. Two fundamental questions must be answered before a suicide request can be considered rational:

- Is the patient able to fully understand his or her disease, prognosis [prediction of outcome], and treatment alternatives?
- Is the patient's depression reversible, given the limitations imposed by the illness, in a way that would substantially alter the circumstances? In other words, is the patient still depressed and desirous of physician-assisted suicide after spiritual, emotional, and physical concerns have been addressed?

If depression seems to be a motivating factor behind a call for physician-assisted suicide, referral of the patient to a psychiatrist for a thorough evaluation is appropriate. A patient may resist psychiatric help for fear of stigmatization. In such cases, the primary care physician may require a psychiatrist's advice.

Offering Palliative Care Alternatives

The vast majority of patients with terminal illnesses can be successfully managed using palliative or comfort care.

This staple of reputable hospice programs is noncurative treatment intended to alleviate symptoms associated with chronic and terminal illnesses. Promoting pastoral, nutritional, and psychological well-being and managing pain are particularly important elements of hospice care. When a patient's suffering is severe enough, a physician may be justified in increasing pain medication, even if the risk of hastening death through the double effect rises as a result.

Stopping life-sustaining therapy such as cardiopulmonary resuscitation (CPR), mechanical ventilation, enteral and parenteral nutrition [nutrition not given by mouth], intravenous (IV) fluids, and hemodialysis [cleaning the blood by machine] is another acceptable palliative intervention, provided the patient is fully informed about the alternatives and has the mental capacity to understand the decision. Families can generally make these decisions on behalf of a patient who has lost mental capacity, provided a clear consensus exists that such actions reflect the patient's values, previously stated wishes, and best interests. Because these decisions frequently result in death, clinicians should be forthright about evaluating such requests, carefully assessing the patient's mental capacity and magnitude of suffering as well as their own knowledge of palliative alternatives.

Placement in a good hospice program that is equipped to care for the needs of the terminally ill is an important step. Hospice programs employ a range of experts skilled in providing physical, emotional, and spiritual care. Although primary care physicians are encouraged to remain involved with the patient until death, they can rely on a team of experts to help resolve end-of-life issues that extend beyond their training and expertise, such as spiritual crises, unresolved issues with family members, or severe depression that requires psychiatric evaluation. If the patient is not eligible for hospice, enlist experts who can provide specialized services based on the patient's most pressing problems. For example, if the patient fears she is not prepared for the afterlife, a chaplain of her religious denomination can be contacted with the patient's consent. If the patient is conflicted because he does not want to financially burden his children, a social worker may be helpful in assessing and resolving the situation.

When Standard Palliative Care Fails

Despite excellent palliative care, a small percentage of patients continue to suffer and continue to request physician-assisted suicide, preferring death to a life burdened with complications of their illnesses. In these cases, some legally acceptable alternatives may be appropriate.

The methods are determined by the patient's clinical situation; the values of the patient, family, and physician; and the status of the law. Knowledge of the range of possibilities can help physicians respond to the relatively rare patients experiencing intolerable pain and suffering without violating their own values or abandoning their patients. The challenge is to find the least harmful alternative.

Recently terminal sedation and voluntary cessation of eating and drinking have been accepted as alternatives for persons whose suffering cannot be alleviated by standard pain management and termination of life support. In 1997 Supreme Court briefs opposing physician-assisted suicide, hospice, palliative care, and geriatric groups stated that terminal sedation and cessation of eating and drinking were morally and clinically preferable last-resort alternatives because death is neither directly nor intentionally hastened by the physician. Some clinicians find these options to be acceptable last resorts in responding to severe terminal suffering.

Voluntary cessation of eating and drinking: By forgoing food and water, fully cognizant patients with terminal or incurable illnesses can achieve a legal and ethical death in a few days or weeks, depending on the underlying disease and the patient's initial metabolic and nutritional states. Like life support, continued nutrition can be classified as an unnecessary means of prolonging an impending death. Although some still consider the act an immoral form of assisted suicide, physicians cannot ethically disregard the wishes of a competent patient who has clearly chosen this method; in fact, the continued feeding and hydration of the patient, whether naturally or artificially, can be considered a form of assault.

Although not directly involved in the implementation of the

patient's decision to forgo eating and drinking, the physician should expect to participate in the initial evaluation and continue to palliate symptoms. The full support of the physician, family and health care team is preferable, as they must continue caring for the patient throughout the dying process. In patients with advanced cancer, hunger is rare and transient and symptoms of dry mouth and throat usually respond to assiduous mouth care.

During the course of dying in this way the patient may become delirious and persistently request a specific food. In this case, it is reasonable to offer it, but if requests for food persist, reevaluate the plan. When patients are considering forgoing food and drink, be sure they understand that terminal delirium may occur toward the very end so you can obtain permission for sedation while the patient is competent.

Terminal sedation: This is a last-resort clinical response to acute, irremediable suffering. Food and fluids are withheld while patients are sedated to the point of unconsciousness and allowed to die of dehydration or complications related to their disease. The dosage of medication is maintained but not increased once sedation is achieved. The primary intent of terminal sedation is to relieve suffering. Terminal sedation is also used regularly in critical care practice to treat symptoms of suffocation in dying patients who are discontinuing mechanical ventilation.

Sedation can be achieved with a barbiturate or benzodiazepine infusion, which should be rapidly increased until the patient is adequately sedated and appears to be comfortable. Possible signs of discomfort include spontaneous stiffening, twitching, and grimacing. When the patient has a good prospect of recovery, continuous sedation usually requires an IV infusion of fluids and even mechanical ventilation. With terminal sedation, however, such life-sustaining measures are withheld since the patient is imminently dying. Both interventions require intensive physician involvement. Opioids [narcotics] for pain and other symptom-relieving measures should be continued to avoid the possibility of unobservable pain or opioid withdrawal, but artificial means of preserving life should be withheld or withdrawn so as not to unnecessarily prolong the dying process.

Talking About Physician-Assisted Suicide

When physicians are unwilling to actively help a patient commit suicide, they must be exceedingly careful to avoid creating a sense of abandonment. If, after a full assessment, the physician cannot prescribe lethal medication, he or she should discuss plans for responding to the patient's condition, including possible cessation of eating and drinking or terminal sedation, if those are acceptable alternatives to both parties. Physicians should assure patients that they will continue to care for them to the best of their ability and skillfully use medications to control pain and other uncomfortable symptoms. Life-long commitment to the dying patient is implicit in such dialogue.

Recommending physician-assisted suicide, cessation of eating and drinking, terminal sedation, or any other potentially life-ending measure to a patient is always contraindicated. Although Oregon physicians can and should inform patients of this and other end-of-life options, promoting physician-assisted suicide as the best intervention borders on coercion. The decision to request a potentially life-ending measure is one that patients must arrive at on their own, after being advised of its risks and benefits and those of all other end-of-life options.

When considering whether to help a patient die through physician-assisted suicide, terminal sedation, stopping a life support measure, or other means, it is essential to get a second opinion from an experienced and trusted colleague. This decision is too serious to be based on the assessment of a single physician. Furthermore, the decision to prescribe lethal medication should never be considered until all other options have been exhausted.

When in doubt, consult with or refer the patient to palliative care specialists. When unaware of the alternatives, physicians and patients often feel helpless. Studies have shown that the more physicians know about palliative care, the less likely they are to view physician-assisted suicide as the only option.

Regardless of the intervention, responding to the patient is imperative, particularly when physician-assisted suicide is not a legal option. Describe the patient's options in a forthright, complete manner. For example: "Maybe terminal sedation is not perfect for you, but it is the best I can do for you right now, and it is better than the intolerable suffering you are experiencing." Finding common ground is usually possible when physicians are willing to be creative and dedicated to nonabandonment.

Family Rights

Ultimately, end-of-life choices should be based on a competent patient's decision. In most cases, however, members of the immediate family should be encouraged to participate in the decision-making process. They must live with the aftermath of the patient's death, and often patients want their families to be involved. A study of patients who legally requested physician-assisted suicide under the Oregon Death with Dignity Act showed that only 13% of them kept their intentions from their family; and in 73% of cases between 1997 and 1999, the attending physician spoke to a family member about the request. Making life and death decisions without input from the patient's family can be a source of enormous conflict.

Occasionally, the patient and family are in staunch opposition regarding treatment options. While the physician's loyalty is to the patient, working to close the gap will help everyone, including the physician. Discussing the patient's wishes and values can help family members appreciate the best course of treatment for that person.

Potential coercion is a problem physicians should be aware of when consulting with family members. For example, if a family member wants to withdraw expensive life-prolonging technology, the situation should be carefully assessed. The same is true of physician-assisted suicide. Although the family usually has the patient's best interests at heart, the request should always be thoroughly evaluated to ensure that carrying out the patient's wishes is everyone's primary goal. If coercion is suspected, confront it, but not before getting verification from a social worker, psychiatrist, and/or a colleague. Never act on any end-of-life request unless it is clearly the patient's.

The Oregon Death with Dignity Act

When it was passed in 1997, the Death with Dignity Act made Oregon the only state in the country to legalize physician-assisted suicide. According to the law, "An adult who is capable, is a resident of Oregon, and has been determined by the attending physician and consulting physician to be suffering from a terminal disease, and who has voluntarily expressed his or her wish to die, may make a written request for medication for the purpose of ending his or her life in a humane and dignified manner in accordance with [The Oregon Death with Dignity Act]." The request must be made both orally and in writing, and the opportunity to rescind at the end of the 15-day waiting period must be offered. Before the prescription is written, the physician verifies that the patient is making an informed decision and is aware of the choice to rescind the request for physician-assisted suicide at any time.

The attending physician has enormous responsibilities before writing a prescription for lethal medication in Oregon. The following provisions of the Death with Dignity Act are guidelines for investigating and carrying out requests for physician-assisted suicide:

- Determine whether the patient has a terminal disease, is capable, and has made an informed and voluntary decision.
- Inform the patient of the medical diagnosis and prognosis, the potential risks and results of taking the lethal medication, and alternatives such as palliative care and hospice care.
- Refer the patient to a consulting physician for medical confirmation of the diagnosis and for a determination that the patient is capable and acting voluntarily.
- Refer the patient for counseling, if appropriate.
- Recommend that the patient notify next of kin.
- Counsel the patient about the importance of having another person present when the prescribed medication is taken and of not taking the medication in a public place.
- Inform the patient of the right to rescind the request at any time and in any manner, and offer an opportunity to rescind at the

end of the 15-day waiting period.
- Verify immediately before writing the prescription for medication, that the patient is making an informed decision.
- Fulfill the medical record documentation requirements.

Legalization: Problem or Solution?

Studies show that in the 42 cases of physician-assisted suicide reported during the Death with Dignity Act's first 2 years of existence, the physicians and patients involved followed all procedures and problems such as vomiting and seizures did not occur. Three of the patients died 11 or more hours after taking their medication, and 1 patient died 23 hours after taking the medication. Deaths due to physician-assisted suicide accounted for 5 and 9 of every 10,000 deaths in Oregon in 1998 and 1999, respectively. Physician-assisted suicide occurs even in states where it is illegal. When the act is forced underground, a physician may tell the patient, "I'm going to give you this bottle of secobarbital, but don't take it all at once, or it can kill you." Underground physician-assisted suicide forces physicians to surreptitiously write prescriptions and abandon the patient at the time of death to avoid prosecution. Legalization allows for open debate, which can lead to discussions about alternatives such as palliative care. But some see the danger of potential abuse with legalization.

Critics of Oregon's legalization of physician-assisted suicide suspect underreporting, technical complications, and the possibility of coercion and active euthanasia. They find support for their theories in recent Dutch studies. A Netherlands analysis of 2 separate studies found that in 18% of the cases, physicians performed euthanasia as a result of complications related to physician-assisted suicide, including problems with completion and the patient's inability to take all the medications. In most of these cases, the patient either did not die as soon as expected or awoke from coma, and the physician felt compelled to administer a lethal injection. In some cases, the physician administered a lethal injection because the patient had difficulty swallowing the oral medication, vomited after swallowing it, or became unconscious before swallowing all of it. Other complications reported in the Netherlands include difficulty inserting an IV line, myoclonus [muscle spasm], and failure to induce coma.

The Pain Relief Promotion Act

In 1997, the Supreme Court decided that physician-assisted suicide is not a constitutional right but that individual states are free to permit it, as did Oregon, or to prohibit it. The pending Pain Relief Promotion Act of 1999, a modified version of the Lethal Drug Abuse Prevention Act of 1998, threatens to severely hamper Oregon's Death with Dignity Act and deter other states from legalizing physician-assisted suicide. Although it would not negate the Death with Dignity Act, this federal act would prohibit physicians from prescribing federally controlled substances for the purpose of ending life or hastening death. The current drug of choice, secobarbital (Seconal), would cease to be a lawful vehicle.

The AMA opposes the legalization of physician-assisted suicide, believing that it threatens both terminally ill patients and physicians' ability to deliver good palliative care. For these reasons, the AMA opposes the Death with Dignity Act and supports the Pain Relief Promotion Act, under which only unintentional death through aggressive palliative care would be protected. Because the bill is not retroactive, physicians who have previously legally assisted a suicide under the Oregon law would not be penalized if it is passed.

Theoretically, the Pain Relief Promotion Act allows for the double effect, but palliative care physicians are skeptical that they would truly be protected. It would be necessary to prove to the Drug Enforcement Administration that their intent in dispensing high dosage medications is to relieve symptoms, not hasten death. As a result of the fear that such tight control would lead to an epidemic of patients dying in acute pain, the bill is widely opposed by the palliative care community, including hospice organizations.

KEVORKIAN: HERO, VILLAIN, OR SOMEWHERE IN BETWEEN?

Timothy E. Quill

Timothy E. Quill, professor of medicine and psychiatry at the University of Rochester (New York), admits that Michigan pathologist Jack Kevorkian, who claims to have helped some 150 people take their own lives, is a controversial figure. Although Quill is a supporter of physician-assisted suicide, he criticizes certain aspects of Kevorkian's actions. At the same time, he points out that Kevorkian's activities have drawn attention to the need for better end-of-life care. Quill was the chief plaintiff in a right-to-die case that the Supreme Court ruled upon in 1997. His numerous writings include *A Midwife Through the Dying Process*.

As an advocate for the open availability of physician-assisted suicide as a last resort, how do I come to grips with the complex issues that Dr. Kevorkian and his wide-ranging activities raise?

Before addressing the question, let me begin with the obvious common ground that Dr. Kevorkian so frequently overlooks. That is the need to improve palliative care. No matter where we stand on the issue of open availability of physician-assisted suicide, we should all work together to support improvements in palliative care. Providing good management of pain and other physical symptoms and giving patients and their families the opportunity to achieve closure to this life in their own way should be the backdrop for all end-of-life care. Hospice programs serve as an excellent model. Such programs, however, are not available to the majority of dying patients for reasons that make no clinical, humanistic, or policy sense. There has been significant movement nationally to improve public awareness about

From "Kevorkian: Hero, Villain, or Somewhere in Between?" by Timothy E. Quill, M.D. This article originally appeared in vol. 8, no. 3, Fall 1999 of *Choices*, the newsletter of Choice in Dying. In March 2000 Choice in Dying evolved into a new organization called Partnership for Caring: America's Voices for the Dying. Partnership for Caring takes no position on physician-assisted suicide or on the passage of the Pain Relief Promotion Act. It advocates for patients' rights to competent medical care, including effective pain management and for universal access to hospice and comprehensive palliative care. If you would like additional information about Partnership for Caring, visit their website www.partnershipforcaring.org or call their toll-free hotline 800-989-9455.

palliative care and to improve its availability. Both advocates and opponents of physician-assisted suicide as a last resort share the common vision of palliative care as the standard of care for people who are dying.

Many who have witnessed harsh death (or who can imagine potentially intolerable end-of-life situations) welcome the promise of palliative care and hospice. But many also want assurance that clinicians would help them to die if they achieve a readiness for death in the face of severe suffering at the end of their life. Most patients will not need such assistance if they receive good palliative care, but the reassurance that there could be an escape can be profoundly comforting. With this comfort, people who had been concerned about potential suffering can spend their limited remaining energy on other more important matters, such as saying goodbye to family and friends. For these individuals, Dr. Kevorkian might be considered a hero—he has dared to be responsive when others in the medical profession have been afraid, and he has openly challenged us all to consider what kinds of choices we would want for ourselves when we are dying.

Ambivalent Reactions

How can people who support more personal choice at the end of life have ambivalence about Dr. Kevorkian? He has clearly raised important questions, and done so in a way that is accessible to media and to pop culture. His suicide machines, videotaped consents by visibly suffering patients, pithy sound bites about a doctor's responsibility to relieve suffering, and courtroom antics are tailor-made for television. His willingness to go to jail for his beliefs, and his readiness to challenge the law and the healthcare professionals who seem so smug in their inclination to ignore tough cases, has garnered the respect of many in the public. His boldness has given the entire end-of-life movement much needed visibility.

Yet there are dark sides to his actions. The ease with which he is willing to act, based on very limited clinical or personal knowledge about the patient, is disturbing. Dr. Kevorkian's primary clinical training and experience is as a pathologist, and he has no training in palliative care, nor has he shown any interest in caring for dying patients who are choosing to continue the struggle to live. The 150 or so "patients" whom he evaluated only superficially before helping end their life included many seemingly compelling cases with well-defined terminal illnesses. But they also included a woman with an "ill-defined uterine condition" and several people who appeared depressed or lacked access to the basics of pain management, much less palliative care.

Although our knowledge of Thomas Youk is limited to the September 1999 "60 Minutes" account, he received euthanasia rather than assisted suicide (which Kevorkian has demonstrated in previous trials is not successfully prosecutable) not because of a compelling clinical need, but because Kevorkian wanted to challenge the law in a new way. The fundamental problem is that the choice of euthanasia was driven by Kevorkian's personal mission and not by Mr. Youk's particular clinical situation. Still, no one else seemed to be willing to be responsive to Mr. Youk's plight, so it seems hypocritical to be too simplistically judgmental.

Too frequently, Dr. Kevorkian presents a stark choice between intolerable suffering and a physician-assisted death, potentially missing the promise of palliative care. But those who believe palliative care has all the answers are also missing a fundamental point—many patients want reassurance that there could be an escape if their suffering gets severe in spite of palliative care. They want to be listened to, and to be given the opportunity to stay in the driver's seat as much as possible during the last chapter of their own life. Kevorkian captures the desire for choice and control that many patients have, but misses the need for relationship and commitment throughout the trials and tribulations of the dying process. The ideal, humane system would include excellent palliative care, committed clinical relationships throughout the dying process, and predictable last resort choices for the really tough cases.

Movement Toward Expansion of Palliative Care

There has been significant movement for those who believe that excellent palliative care must include a predictable way to escape if and when suffering becomes intolerable. The following are some examples.

The first year experience in Oregon, where physician-assisted death has been legally available subject to safeguards since 1997, has exploded many of the myths about the danger of such practices.

Witness the following:

- Of an estimated 29,000 deaths in the state, there were only 15 cases of physician-assisted deaths; all 15 had access to good palliative care and none cited financial concerns.
- Referrals to hospice increased (Oregon's referrals are twice the national average); prescribing for pain improved (Oregon consistently ranks among the highest states for per capita prescribing of opioid pain medication); and more patients died at home where most people want to die.
- Pain was rarely the sole reason for requesting this assistance; more commonly other physical symptoms in combination with the fear of loss of autonomy and independence in the last phases of dying influenced that decision.
- Many more patients sought reassurance that there could be an escape than actually ended their life using this method.

While we are learning about the real, rather than the hypothetical, impact of the legalization of physician-assisted suicide in Oregon, there is increasing discussion within palliative care circles about other last resort options if suffering becomes intolerable. Two such practices are terminal sedation and voluntarily stopping eating and drinking. Although these options have considerable moral or clinical complexity, they have the advantage of not requiring changes in the law. They are also acceptable to many clinicians and patients who oppose other forms of physician-assisted death. These last resort possibilities have not been included in any polls in the United States about physician-assisted death. Yet each intimately involves physicians and should be subject to safeguards similar to those proposed for physician-assisted suicide. Because legal codification is not needed for these practices—unlike physician-assisted suicide, we can create safeguards in the form of guidelines, rather than regulation, allowing for much-needed flexibility. . . .

Defeat of Lethal Drug Abuse Prevention Act

A broad coalition of organizations with common interest in improving care at the end of life worked together to defeat the Hyde-Nichols bill in Congress in 1998. This bill would have allowed the federal government to intervene in Oregon's affairs by indirectly criminalizing physicians whose "intent" when prescribing controlled substances was in compliance with Oregon's Death With Dignity Act. If enacted, the bill would have undermined adequate treatment of pain across the country by involving the Drug Enforcement Agency (DEA) in legitimate medical practices and making the legal risks of prescribing opioid pain relievers seem even greater than they already do. A new version of the same legislation (The Pain Relief Promotion Act) was reintroduced in June 1999, with tempting increased support for palliative care, but still with unprecedented and frightening DEA oversight of physician prescribing practices.

I hope members of the coalition will not be tempted by this complex legislation, which risks so much in terms of undermining pain management and overriding the decision of Oregon voters. Imagine, if you will, DEA regulators or local prosecutors evaluating a physician's intent in prescribing high dose opioids or providing terminal sedation for a patient with accelerating symptoms toward the end of life. The progress we have made overcoming the climate of legal fear inhibiting these practices would be severely undermined with the passage of the so-called "Pain Relief Promotion" Act.

In the final analysis, Dr. Kevorkian symbolically speaks to the issue of choice without responsibility. Potentially life-ending decisions, such as stopping life support, giving terminal sedation, or physician-assisted suicide, should be made only as a last resort, with great respect for the life that is ending. Before acting, clinicians must ensure that optimal palliative care is available, that the decision is not being distorted by mental illness or coerced by social pressures, and that there are no less harmful ways to proceed. The doctor-patient relationship must always include the doctor's commitment to care for the patient and family no matter what decision is ultimately made. It is only in the context of excellent care and commitment that these heart-wrenching last resort decisions can make moral and clinical sense for physicians.

THE JUSTIFICATION FOR IMPRISONING KEVORKIAN

Jessica Cooper

On March 26, 1999, a jury convicted Jack Kevorkian of second-degree murder for injecting a lethal drug into Thomas Youk, who had an incurable illness and had asked Kevorkian for help in dying. Jessica Cooper, a circuit court judge in Oakland, Michigan, presided at Kevorkian's trial. In this statement, made on April 13 when she sentenced Kevorkian to 10 to 25 years in prison, Cooper says that Kevorkian's defiance of the legal system was the chief factor in determining his sentence. Whatever his feelings about physician-assisted death, she claims, he cannot place himself "above the law."

This is a court of law and you said you invited yourself here to take a final stand. But this trial was not an opportunity for a referendum. The law prohibiting euthanasia was specifically reviewed and clarified by the Michigan Supreme Court several years ago in a decision involving your very own cases, sir.

So the charge here [of murder] should come as no surprise to you. You invited yourself to the wrong forum.

Well, we are a nation of laws, and we are a nation that tolerates differences of opinion because we have a civilized and a nonviolent way of resolving our conflicts. That way is the law and adherence to the law.

We have the means and the methods to protest the laws with which we disagree. You can criticize the law, you can write or lecture about the law, you can speak to the media or petition the voters.

But you must always stay within the limits provided by the law. You may not break the law. You may not take the law into your own hands.

In point of fact, the issue of assisted suicide was addressed in this state by referendum in November 1998. And while the proponents of that were out campaigning, you were with Thomas Youk. And the voters of the state of Michigan said "no." And they said no two-and-a-half to one.

But we are not talking about assisted suicide here. When you purposely inject another human being with what you know to be a lethal dose of poison, that, sir, is murder. And the jury so found.

Compassion—or Defiance of the Law?

Now, you've vilified the jury and the justice system in this case.

But every member of that jury had compassion and empathy for Thomas Youk. They had a higher duty that went beyond personal sympathy and emotion. They took an oath to follow the law, not to nullify it.

And I am bound by a very similar oath, sir.

No one is unmindful of the controversy and emotion that exists over end-of-life issues and pain control. And I assume that the debate will continue in a calm and reasoned forum long after this trial and your activities have faded from public memory.

But this trial is not about that controversy. The trial was about you, sir. It was about you and the legal system. And you have ignored and challenged the legislature and the Supreme Court. And moreover, you've defied your own profession, the medical profession.

You stood before this jury and you spoke of your duty as a physician. You repeatedly speak of treating patients to relieve their pain and suffering. You don't have a license to practice medicine. The state of Michigan told you eight years ago you may not practice medicine. You may not treat patients. You may not possess—let alone administer or inject—drugs into another human being.

Now, the reason the guidelines [for sentencing] in this particular case are so high is because of the drug conviction in Count 2. And everyone seems to have glossed over this particular offense. But you had no right to be in control of any type of a controlled substance, let alone deliver it to anyone else.

There are several valid considerations in sentencing. One of them is rehabilitation.

But based upon the fact that you've publicly and repeatedly announced your intentions to disregard the laws of this state, I question whether you will ever cease and desist. The fact that your attorney in a presentence investigation says you're out of business from this point forward doesn't negate your past statements.

Now, another consideration and perhaps even a stronger factor in sentencing is deterrence. This trial was not about the political or moral correctness of euthanasia. It was all about you, sir. It was about lawlessness. It was about disrespect for a society that exists and flourishes because of the strength of the legal system.

No one, sir, is above the law. No one.

So let's talk just a little more about you specifically.

You were on bond to another judge when you committed this offense, you were not licensed to practice medicine when you committed this offense and you hadn't been licensed for eight years. And you had the audacity to go on national television, show the world what you did and dare the legal system to stop you. Well, sir, consider yourself stopped.

CHAPTER 3

EUTHANASIA AND THE LAW

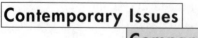

ASSISTED SUICIDE SHOULD BE LEGALIZED

Sanford Levinson

In this selection, Sanford Levinson, an expert on constitutional law, discusses what he feels should be the liberal response to the U.S. Supreme Court's unanimous decision in June 1997 that terminally ill patients do not have a constitutional right to ask their physicians for assistance in suicide. Levinson believes that physician-assisted suicide for terminally ill people should be legalized, but he stresses that liberals must recognize the dangers that legalization might present to the aged and vulnerable groups. Levinson is a professor of the School of Law at the University of Texas, Austin, and has been a visiting professor at Yale Law School.

Do doctors have a constitutional right to prescribe drugs for their patients that will be used, if at all, only when the patients decide to commit suicide? Both the Ninth and Second Circuit Appeals Courts, though with different legal theories, said yes in 1996. Although the Supreme Court rejected those rulings unanimously in June 1997 and found that the Constitution contains no such right, discussion will scarcely cease. Four of the nine Justices went out of their way to emphasize the narrowness of the ruling, interpreting the decision as involving only a highly general "right to assisted suicide." While agreeing that the Constitution contains no such unlimited right, they strongly suggested that the result would be different had a suit been carefully limited to consideration of a specific claim by a person suffering great pain or debilitation in the terminal stages of an illness. A fifth Justice, David Souter, who wrote the most legally thoughtful opinion of them all, also seemed to leave the door open for possible reconsideration.

The Liberal Response

Dr. Samuel Johnson was of course right in saying that the prospect of one's death concentrates the mind. What ought to be the state's role in determining how we die? Is there a recognizably "liberal" (or "conservative") response to this question?

Reprinted, with permission, from Sanford Levinson, "The Court's Death Blow," *The Nation*, July 21, 1997. Copyright © 1997 The Nation Company Inc.

The answer is easy only if one makes "liberalism" synonymous with "libertarianism," an ever-more-influential philosophy limiting the state to its classical night-watchman functions of providing police protection against criminals, defense against foreign enemies and enforcement of contracts voluntarily agreed to by consenting adults. These classical liberals are, of course, usually described as conservatives within contemporary American politics. Popular liberalism (or "progressivism," a term coming back into fashion by persons who, for whatever reason, are uncomfortable with the term "liberalism") has for more than a century been defined in large measure by rejecting the libertarian emphasis on "freedom of contract," which justifies, for example, the right of employers to exact whatever terms they can from their workers, thus legitimizing minimum-wage or maximum-hour laws.

Liberals not only reject indifference to the potential for exploitation; they have also condemned any reading of the Constitution that would protect such libertarian principles against what the Court once termed the "meddlesome interferences" of the legislature. This phrase comes from *Lochner v. New York*, the 1905 decision that read the Constitution as a substantially libertarian document invalidating a New York maximum-hour law. Lochner's specter has dominated U.S. constitutional theory for almost a century. In an extraordinarily influential dissent, Justice Oliver Wendell Holmes rejected libertarianism as a constitutionally embedded principle and proclaimed the "right of a majority to embody their opinions in law." Holmes's dissent was proudly affirmed by most liberals, who used it to justify the obliteration of any constitutionally protected "freedom of contract."

But "freedom of contract" sometimes reappears even within the liberal litany of concerns. One is abortion, which can be analyzed as the claim that a woman and her doctor should be constitutionally protected in regard to any contract that they might choose to reach. Similarly, the "assisted suicide" argument can also easily be described in freedom-of-contract (and "pro-choice") terms. Can a doctor in effect enter into a contract to provide the particular assistance that is sought? It is important to note that no one argues that doctors must adhere to their patients' wishes to make available potentially fatal doses of noncurative drugs.

Two questions, then, must be addressed by any liberal. The first is philosophical: What ought the state to do when faced with the desire of a doctor to comply with a patient's request for a prescription of a life-ending drug? This boils down to asking how one would vote in a legislature or, if one is a citizen of one of the Western states, in a public referendum. (Assisted suicide proposals were voted down in California and Washington but approved in Oregon, though the Oregon legislature in early June 1997 passed a measure putting the issue back before the public in a new referendum.) But referendums are beside the point if a second question—does the Constitution substantially remove this issue from the electorate?—is answered in the affirmative.

Dangers of Legalization

While I would vote to allow the doctor-patient "contracts" I have described, I would do so with ambivalence. Many of the opponents of such legislation make arguments quite similar to standard-form liberal reasoning with which I am usually sympathetic. The most eloquent of the anti-assistance briefs submitted to the Supreme Court was written by University of Utah law professor Michael McConnell, on behalf of Senator Orrin Hatch and Representatives Henry Hyde and Charles Canady. One should resist a temptation to label this the "conservatives' brief," for most of its arguments focus on what liberals like to think is their patented concern for the fate of the most vulnerable among us. One can scarcely dismiss the plausible fear that those who are sick will be subtly encouraged to "choose" death if assisted suicide becomes a widely recognized option. If they are poor, and especially if they are receiving subsidized care, that pressure may well come from doctors who are internalizing the concern about costs that increasingly drives American medicine. If they are well-off, the pressure might instead come from children who are aware of how useful it would be to have the estate to pay for their own needs instead of for "futile" medical care.

Defenders of assisted suicide, such as the "dream team" of philosophers who submitted a brief to the Supreme Court, recognize the existence of this problem but basically minimize its importance, preferring instead to occupy the high theoretical ground of personal autonomy as a transcendent value. They also note that many of the same fears can be encountered in regard to the now well-recognized right of people to withdraw from life support or to reject medical treatment *tout court* [without explanation]. Ironically, for some readers this comparison may serve more to shake their confidence in existing doctrine than lead them to accept its considerable expansion to the realm of assisted suicide.

As the philosophers point out, the concerns expressed are basically "paternalistic," premised on the view that a person might not genuinely be the judge of his or her own best interest. Libertarian-oriented liberals resist paternalistic regulation. But the philosophers, like all defenders of the "pro-choice" position in regard to death, are extremely eager to emphasize how they would in fact limit effective choice only to those deemed sufficiently mentally healthy after examinations by teams of psychiatrists and doctors. In answer to the question asked by playwright Brian Clark some years ago, *Whose Life Is It Anyway?*, almost no one is truly willing to say, "The person's own, to do with as he or she wishes." That answer evokes the image of a medical emergency unit feeling honor-bound to obey the following note

written by a 20-year-old: "I cannot go on after losing my true love. I
have taken an overdose of sleeping pills. Do not revive me if you find
me before I am dead." Since almost no one defends honoring that
person's autonomy, the answer to Clark's question turns out to be,
"Your life is really the property of professionals, usually psychiatrists,
who will decide whether your reasons for wishing to die are really
good enough."

Thus, even those defending a constitutional right to assisted suicide would ultimately license a great deal of state interference in the
process surrounding death—more, indeed, than may currently occur.
Almost everyone agrees that assisted suicide (and euthanasia) occurs,
though outside the penetrating gaze of the law. As Guido Calabresi
and Philip Bobbitt argued some years ago in their aptly named *Tragic
Choices*, there are some decisions that are probably best made out of
that gaze. It is impossible both to envision precisely what regulatory
schemes would follow a decision to "legalize" assisted suicide and to
be confident that patients would actually be better off.

Consider, for example, a legal regime that effectively limits assisted
suicide to those who are "terminally ill." If taken seriously, this would
mean that a doctor could not supply fatal dosages of drugs to persons
faced with ten years of unremitting pain, whereas someone with a
prognosis of only six months would be eligible. This makes no sense
and underscores why the rhetorical emphasis on the terminally ill,
found in the concurring opinions of Justices Sandra Day O'Connor,
John Paul Stevens and Souter, is in fact misleading.

Who Should Decide?

Still, these questions go to philosophy and political ideology. The
more important issue to constitutional lawyers is whether the Constitution has already made that decision for us. The Court has said the
answer is no, at least if the question is asked very broadly. Were the
Justices wrong? It is difficult to extract such a decision (which could
take the form of saying either that the state must always tolerate
assisted suicide or that the state cannot tolerate it at all, as has been
argued by opponents of the Oregon law) from the unadorned text,
history or structure of the Constitution. The best legal arguments
come from effectively milking certain decisions—including *Planned
Parenthood of Southeastern Pennsylvania v. Casey* (1992)—that reaffirmed basic rights of choice concerning reproduction.

One might simply swallow hard and support judicial decision-making in this area if one believed that the case involved the rights of a
vulnerable minority likely to be ignored or otherwise devalued by the
ordinary political process. Although Laurence Tribe, in his own brief to
the Court on assisted suicide, made a valiant effort to analogize those
seeking physician assistance in dying to more traditional minorities,
he is ultimately unpersuasive. All of us are going to die, whereas only a

minority of us are, say, African-Americans or Jehovah's Witnesses.

Nor is the issue like that of abortion, where one can be confident that the males who dominate state legislatures never have to worry about being pregnant themselves. Every member of the legislature should be able to envision the possibility of being desperately ill and pleading with a doctor for prescriptions that will enable him or her to die. And members of legislatures should also be able to envision, perhaps by examining their feelings about their aged and highly vulnerable parents, the pressures that might be brought to bear on them to exit this vale of tears. Lawmakers thus have every incentive to think with extreme seriousness about the issues involved.

So, on balance, what should "liberals" believe in regard to assisted suicide? With fear and trembling, we should, as a political matter, support enhancing the choices available to people (including, ultimately, to us) as death begins to overtake life. But we should also recognize that people of undoubted good faith, committed no less than we are to protecting the vulnerable and to criticizing optimistic assumptions about "free markets" and "untrammeled choice," are on the other side of this issue. It is a true judgment call, balancing important autonomy interests against the possibility of exploitation. Finally, it is hard to see why the extremely important social and political conversation that is only now emerging should be foreclosed by an extraordinarily controversial reading of the Constitution that would, among other things, substantially increase state regulation of the process of death in entirely unpredictable ways. There is no reason, then, even for staunch liberals to bewail the Court's decision on assisted suicide, especially given the de facto majority's apparent willingness to revisit the issue should, for example, a state actually prosecute, and a jury convict, a doctor for prescribing fatal doses of a drug to a terminally ill patient facing excruciating pain.

ASSISTED SUICIDE SHOULD BE ILLEGAL

James F. Breshnahan

James F. Breshnahan states that fellow opponents of the legalization of physician-assisted suicide should be pleased with the June 1997 U.S. Supreme Court's ruling that the Constitution does not include a right to ask for assistance in suicide. He asserts that the justices' reasoning affirms arguments against legalization of assisted suicide. However, he warns, their statements leave room for assistance in suicide to be legally permitted under some circumstances. Breshnahan is a professor at the Northwestern University Medical School in Chicago.

The U.S. Supreme Court announced on June 26, 1997, unanimous decisions in the cases *Washington v. Glucksberg* and *Vacco v. Quill*. All nine Justices agreed in rejecting claims previously accepted by two Federal circuit courts of appeal; they denied that assistance by physicians in suicide is a constitutionally protected right of terminally ill persons and their physicians. But how real was the unanimity among the nine Justices? In fact, differences of viewpoint expressed in the several opinions of the Justices in these cases present us with a continuing challenge: Take better care of the dying.

This challenge is addressed both to those who advocate and those who oppose physician assistance to a terminally ill person in inflicting death on himself or herself to end suffering—PAD (the acronym for the euphemism, "physician-assisted dying"). The challenge will, of course, be perceived differently by proponents and opponents of PAD. Yet I believe that both sides can and should recognize a common ground for shared effort to enhance and broaden access to palliative medicine and hospice care in order to respond to the needs of the terminally ill.

Support for Bans on Assisted Suicide

At first reading, the unanimity of the court and the arguments made by Chief Justice Rehnquist in the majority opinions in these two cases may tempt opponents of PAD to rest on their oars. After all, don't these opinions unambiguously reaffirm the traditionally accepted difference and so a distinction between PAD as "killing" and the practice of palliation as "letting die"?

The majority opinions by the Chief Justice are joined directly by Justices Antonin Scalia, Clarence Thomas and Anthony Kennedy, and joined as well by Justice Sandra Day O'Connor in a single concurring opinion (applicable to both cases) that is joined by Justice Ruth Bader Ginsburg. Chief Justice William Rehnquist's opinions not only affirm the validity of the distinction between permitting death to occur and inflicting death but rehearse the long-standing rejection of assistance to suicide to be found in U.S. common law. These opinions also accept as valid the justifications advanced for criminalizing PAD by Washington State and New York: to prevent predictable harm to 5 individuals and to society that would result from the practice of PAD.

First, in *Quill v. Vacco*, the Chief Justice explains how PAD is legally and morally different from medical practices of letting die both in the intention of the actors and in the causality of their actions. He argues that this is so whether letting die is accomplished through foregoing so-called life-prolonging treatments, or through letting a terminal disease process progress in combination with possible (but in fact rare) lethal side effects of using needed pain-relieving measures. (Use of analgesics involves some risk of accelerating death, and this can be foreseen but not directly intended when doctors try to measure the dose necessary to relieve pain and suffering.) The decisions of the two circuit courts of appeal had rejected this distinction, insisting that these two forms of letting die and PAD are now merely variations of a single growing practice of "hastening death."

Rejecting that view, the Chief Justice notes that the distinction here reaffirmed lies at the heart of all common law definitions of crime. In PAD one unambiguously intends a death-causing act to take effect and one initiates a new lethal process different from the disease or injury processes that make the patient terminal. So the causal involvement is proximate, not remote, even though in PAD it is done by cooperation of physicians with a patient's self-inflicted death rather than by the physician's own action (as in euthanasia).

Of course, the Chief Justice recognizes that both of these forms of "letting die" can be abused. A doctor can really intend to kill but disguise this by pretending to do what can be, in moral intention, an honest acceptance of an unwanted side effect, namely death. A doctor can, for instance, deliberately but covertly overdose a dying patient with analgesia. Or a doctor can forego further use of cure-oriented treatments, even though they and their patients do not reasonably judge these to be excessively burdensome. Such possibilities of homicidal abuse may often be difficult to prove, but the validity of the distinction between killing and letting die is not obliterated by that. In PAD, it remains easy to observe and prove both homicidal intention and causality.

So we who oppose PAD are encouraged. Six Justices have agreed that, from both a moral and legal point of view, one can act in a way that is not homicidal—sometimes to stop what is now an unreasonable medical interference with human dying, sometimes to take risks to relieve suffering. Doctors can do so because they recognize an urgent moral duty to take greater risks of unwanted but sometimes inevitable side effects of their interventions because those risks are proportionally justified where death is already at hand. They can proceed sensibly to tailor medical interventions in a way that is appropriate to the close approach of a normal human event, dying, without resort to inflicting death. Justice O'Connor's crucial concurring opinion in the Nancy Cruzan case (decided in 1988) foretelling a constitutional right of the dying to control their medical treatment is here re-enforced. Only homicide and suicide are here excluded from medical practice.

Need for Better Palliative Care

In addition, the Chief Justice's majority opinion in *Washington v. Glucksberg* persuasively elaborates the constitutionally valid reasons a state has for continuing to make PAD subject to criminal penalties. The states act reasonably when they anticipate harms from allowing PAD. These possible harms include: danger of undermining policies discouraging suicides due to psychological impairment, and other laws against homicide as well; danger to the ethics of the profession of medicine, whether from evasion of the restraints on the practice of PAD that all admit the states have a right to impose on doctors, or from an inevitable devolution of practice from assisting suicide to actively inflicting death at the request of those patients unable to do so themselves; danger of family participation with or in place of doctors in suicide by the terminally ill; and with all of these, danger of various kinds of coercion especially of vulnerable patients leading to less than free requests for PAD once it has become a legally accepted medical practice. These harms are reasonably foreseen and criminal penalties are reasonably crafted by a state to prevent them.

Such arguments of the majority opinions can surely hearten those who oppose PAD. But, in spite of the apparent weight of argument against PAD, and apart from the influence this may have in discouraging state legislatures from enacting laws legalizing PAD, none of this judicial reasoning contributes directly to what is most important for dying patients. These two majority opinions do not of themselves generate efforts to foster a growth in good and appropriate use of palliative medicine and hospice-type care for those dying under medical care. That is the crucial challenge for those who claim to oppose PAD.

To understand our need to attend to this challenge, we must carefully examine the separate concurring opinions of the other five Justices.

First, consider the very succinct concurring opinion of Justice

O'Connor, which Justice Ginsberg simply joins, and with which Justice Steven Breyer expresses agreement except insofar as it joins the majority opinion. Only here do we find explicit mention of alternative opportunities in current medical practice for relief of suffering available to the dying. We begin to confront some indication of possible reservations about the tenor of the majority opinions on the part of at least four and perhaps six Justices.

Justice O'Connor insists that, beside seeking to avoid the harms enumerated by the Chief Justice, the states are not to make legally unavailable to dying patients who endure great suffering the adequate palliative medical means of relieving that suffering. This, in her view, is an important justification for a state in making PAD illegal. She states explicitly:

> The parties and amici agree that in these states a patient who is suffering from a terminal illness and who is experiencing great pain has no legal barriers to obtaining medication from qualified physicians to alleviate that suffering, even to the point of causing unconsciousness and hastening death.

Justice O'Connor does not state that such appropriate palliative medical care of the dying is readily available in practice. She does not claim that it is frequently and effectively given. She only emphasizes that as long as effective palliative care is not forbidden by law, by state action, no constitutional right to PAD can be claimed as the only effective means of controlling one's death when suffering is great. The majority opinions failed to include this observation. So it appears that this justification of the state's outlawing of PAD is for her, and for Justice Ginsberg as well, more than a casual afterthought. Stating it is necessary for them to be able to join in the majority opinions.

Second, in his single concurring opinion (applicable to both cases), Justice Breyer probes the practical medical problem of limited availability of palliative care—that it is still very infrequently provided, or even offered, to dying patients. This issue appears to weigh against his endorsing the majority opinions of the Chief Justice. Justice Breyer expresses concern that the predicament of the dying is not fully and realistically taken into account by the majority opinions in these two cases, even though he concurs in the outcomes.

Third, Justice David Souter in his two concurring opinions explicitly refuses to join the majority opinions. At considerable length he develops a different way of determining whether the claim of a 14th Amendment right can be made and whether a state has sufficient reasons to limit or deny that right claimed. He requires a careful and detailed weighing of the claims of rights of the dying and their doctors against the dangers for the prevention of which states claim a need to forbid PAD. In the end, this weighing of claims of right against claims of preventing harm leads him to accept the decisions in these particular cases. But he appears to accept, in a way the majority does not, the strong case that might be made for a right of some terminally ill persons to have assistance in ending unendurable suffering by self-inflicted death.

Fourth, though he concurs in these two decisions, in his single concurring opinion Justice John Paul Stevens expresses forthright reservations about the scope of the holdings. Indeed, in his arguments he appears very close to writing a dissent. He, more emphatically than the other four concurring Justices, recognizes a right to control the circumstances of one's dying, and so he anticipates cases in which better arguments for a constitutional right to PAD could well be made by doctors and patients in particularly difficult circumstances. Justice Stevens states that he might well evaluate such arguments in a way that will qualify or even reverse the decisions in these two cases.

Profound Differences

Thus, Justices Stevens, Souter and Breyer are much less than irrevocably committed to the votes they have cast in these two cases against a constitutional right to PAD. They indicate in different ways that the needs of the dying for appropriate relief of suffering must receive more explicit attention than the Chief Justice and his three colleagues have accorded them.

And by indicating the crucial role in their votes played by their concern that dying persons not be legally denied access to adequate medical relief of suffering, Justices O'Connor and Ginsberg may be positioned at least partway on the road to forming a new majority of five Justices. For instance, they might vote differently if it were demonstrated to them that some form of government action in fact presents a barrier to the effective practice of palliative medicine in the care of the dying.

Since these five Justices might reconsider the holdings in these two cases denying constitutional protection to claims of a right to PAD, the apparent unanimity of the Supreme Court could turn out to be a short-lasting papering-over of profound differences. Opponents of PAD have not won the war by this decision, perhaps not even a decisive battle in this war, possibly only a preliminary skirmish.

From the point of view of traditional medical morality and Catholic moral analysis, the majority opinions of the Chief Justice and the three Justices who join directly in his opinion seem to me too much preoccupied with ruling out homicide in care of the dying in a merely legalistic way. They express too little insight into the realities of medical experience, to what medical people experience as they struggle against a previously dominant medical vitalism in order to care well for the dying. Preoccupied with simply excluding homicide and suicide, the Chief Justice and his three colleagues fail to take into account that this medical vitalism continues to cause too many physicians actually to oppose use of palliative medicine and hospice care and to seek to "prolong life" at whatever cost the patient must bear in suffering and expense. They ignore the harm that this medical vitalism has perpetrated in the name of a war against death and the role this has played in fostering claims to the right to have PAD.

By contrast, Justice Breyer, and in some lesser degree Justices O'Connor and Ginsberg, show informed insight into these realities of medical experience of the needs of the dying in a high-technology medical system—an insight very rarely displayed in previous judicial opinions. This appears to be the result of several amicus curiae briefs that were devoted to elaborating a picture of current practice in care of the dying and its limitations. Justice Souter's style of constitutional analysis appears designed to give great weight to such insight in future cases. And Justice Stevens seems eager to take this insight fully into account if a stronger case is made for desperate needs of dying patients.

I believe that the opinions of these five Justices give no cause for opponents of PAD to rest on their oars, and give every reason for those who seek better care of the dying to renew their dedication to this challenge.

Open Door for Physician-Assisted Suicide Death

The challenge to those who advocate PAD is obvious enough. The majority opinions of Chief Justice Rehnquist, as well as the concurring opinion of Justice O'Connor joined by Justice Ginsberg, offer hope for eventual victory through legislation. These six Justices say that state legislatures remain the appropriate forum in which the dispute about the moral appropriateness and practical feasibility of decriminalizing, and so permitting, some kind of carefully constrained physician assistance in self-inflicted death by the terminally ill can be examined and, perhaps, be experimented with. The other three separately concurring Justices, Souter, Breyer and Stevens, in no way deny this invitation.

In Oregon, where a ballot initiative permitting PAD had already been passed by a narrow vote of the general electorate in 1994, we may witness the first experiment with open practice of PAD. "May"— because the Oregon legislature mandated a second vote on this measure in the 1997 general election. (The legislature is, perhaps, concerned that Oregon, as the only state with such a law, will become a resort for terminally ill persons seeking assisted suicide.) A decision of the 9th Federal Circuit Court of Appeals (*Lee v. Oregon*, 1997) upholding the constitutionality of this Oregon law has recently been denied review by the U.S. Supreme Court and is thus left in effect. Of course, since the Oregon electorate ratified this law again in November 1997, the Supreme Court may eventually reconsider the constitutionality of that statute. Not until the law is put into practice will we have concrete experience of the impact on medical practice of PAD, especially on the rights of vulnerable patients. If harms from such practice become manifest, a new case challenging the constitutionality of PAD might win review and a majority of the present Justices.

However practice evolves in Oregon, the advocates of PAD can be expected to accept the express invitation of the Justices in *Glucksberg* and *Quill* to continue to advance their cause within the other 49 state legislative assemblies of our nation. Nonetheless, I believe that proponents of PAD are genuinely concerned about the plight of dying patients; they should and will be willing also to work hard to advance the cause of good palliative medicine and hospice care. Almost all of the physician proponents have proclaimed their support for such care, even as something that would be required before accepting a patient's request for PAD. They advocate decriminalizing PAD because they claim it is needed as a last resort only in rare cases.

Good and Effective Care of the Dying

What should we expect in the next stage of our North American struggle to provide good care of the dying? I believe it is time for all who have any true sense of compassion toward the dying, and who expect to receive compassionate care when they themselves are dying, to work unremittingly to foster adequate practice of palliative medical care of the dying and wider and wider practice of a constantly improved hospice care of the dying. And governmentally reimbursed programs such as Medicare and Medicaid must be led decisively into the fold—they are not there yet. We have a chance now to make support of hospice care of the dying a sine qua non of all health insurance. We are challenged now to make this hospice practice available to all the dying who are without health care coverage—as Mother Teresa did so compassionately for the destitute of India and elsewhere.

Above all, people involved in health care have now what may be a brief window of opportunity to increase their efforts to improve and refine palliative medicine and hospice practice so that fewer and fewer persons imagine that PAD is their only hope, as they live in fear of unrelieved suffering and indignity in their dying as a consequence of medical neglect. The various hospice programs strongly emphasize not only exquisite attention to relieving the suffering of the dying but also, perhaps most important of all, to supporting the dying persons in their need to care for their caregivers as a final expression of their life values.

Unfortunately, some vociferous opponents of PAD tell us little about what they want, affirmatively, to do for the dying. That is the fatal weakness that I am convinced will destroy their efforts to prevent legalization of PAD in state legislatures. If what they really want is merely the status quo—a sterile medical vitalism—they doom their own cause. More serious from a moral standpoint, that approach fails in the solemn obligation we have to provide dying persons the sort of realistic and compassionate caring that they need in the final moments of their life's journey.

We who are Christian believers must now embrace the challenge to action, to an orthopraxis that matches our orthodox moral belief in compassionate caring for the dying. We believe that, in the final moments of living, we and those for whom we care are being drawn into the dying of Christ. That is a supreme moment for love and compassion, by caregivers of the dying and by the dying for their caregivers.

ASSISTED SUICIDE SHOULD BE RESTRICTED TO THE TERMINALLY ILL

Martin Gunderson and David J. Mayo

In this selection, Martin Gunderson and David J. Mayo explain why they believe that physician-assisted death should be legalized but restricted to the terminally ill, at least for now. The incurably but not terminally ill, they say, might benefit just as much from assisted death, but this group's risks from legalization would be much greater than those of the terminally ill. Martin Gunderson is a professor of philosophy at Macalester College in St. Paul, Minnesota. David J. Mayo is a professor of philosophy at the University of Minnesota, Duluth, and a faculty associate of the University of Minnesota Center for Bioethics.

The last twenty years have seen a significant shift in the debate over physician-assisted death. Earlier opposition appealed primarily to either the sanctity of life or the preservation of life as the defining goal of medicine. Today most opposition focuses on the dangers it might pose, either through error or coercion in particular cases, or through the gradual lifting of initial restrictions and a subsequent slide down a slippery slope of public policy.

Supporters of physician-assisted death, the present authors among them, acknowledge that there are dangers and have proposed a variety of safeguards. These include second opinions of diagnoses, psychological consultation to ensure that the patient is of sound mind and is not suffering from a treatable depression, checks to ensure that the patient is both fully informed and not being coerced, and a "cooling off" period to ensure that the patient's judgment is a considered one. The safeguards attempt to restrict physician aid-in-dying to those it would genuinely benefit and to protect vulnerable persons for whom it might otherwise pose a risk of harm. But while advocates intend to draw a reasonable line on a continuum of possible policies that vary with respect to both their potential benefits and their risks, to critics the safeguards are a vain attempt to get a toehold on a dangerous slope that will ultimately provide no toeholds.

Reprinted from "Restricting Physician-Assisted Death to the Terminally Ill," by Martin Gunderson and David J. Mayo, *Hastings Center Report,* November 2000. Copyright © 2000. Reprinted with permission.

A Controversial Requirement

One safeguard—that physician-assisted death be restricted to the terminally ill—has proven to be especially controversial even among supporters of physician-assisted death. It is worthwhile exploring this safeguard not only because it is controversial, but also because of the light it sheds on slippery slope arguments against physician-assisted death. The arguments against the terminal illness requirement illustrate the force of gravity that pulls policy on physician-assisted death down the slope, and attempts to answer those objections force us to deal with problems of line-drawing on the slope.

The terminal illness requirement is a prominent part of Oregon's Death with Dignity Act, the proposed Maine Death with Dignity Act, and initiatives that were defeated in Washington, California, and Michigan. In his recent book, *A Midwife through the Dying Process*, Timothy Quill also recommends that physician aid-in-dying be made available only to those who are terminally ill. However, not all advocates of physician-assisted death favor this safeguard. In the Netherlands, physician-assisted death is available to those who have irremediable and severe suffering whether or not they are terminally ill. The Harvard Model Law would allow physician-assisted death for people who have an intractable and unbearable illness as well as for people who are terminally ill. Even Quill himself once argued that the requirement of terminal illness would "arbitrarily exclude people with incurable, but not imminently terminal, progressive illness such as ALS or multiple sclerosis."

Four main arguments have been advanced by those who oppose the requirement that someone receiving physician-assisted death be terminally ill. The first two arguments invoke compassion and self-determination, respectively, and suggest that the reasons for supporting physician-assisted death apply to nonterminal and terminal patients alike. The third argument goes on to conclude that restricting physician-assisted death to those who are terminally ill would therefore be arbitrary and hence unfair. The fourth argument concerns vagueness.

The Argument from Compassion

Compassion is often cited as a reason for physician-assisted death. As compassionate persons, we want to enhance others' well-being and help minimize pointless suffering. Thus physicians' duties are not limited to curing and treating, but include also alleviating the suffering of those beyond the reach of effective treatment. Unfortunately, terminal illness can involve horrible suffering, including mental anguish that is beyond the scope of even optimal palliative care. There is good evidence that people who have sought physician-assisted death have been motivated by anguish—over, for example, their loss of dignity or loss of control—even more than by physical pain. Eric Cassell has suggested that perhaps the most terrible feature of illness generally is not that it causes pain but that it compromises our control over our lives. As control ebbs away, terminally ill patients may fear the disintegration not only of their bodies but of their very selves, understood as agents-in-the-world. While doubtless much more can and should be done to attend not just to the physical but also to the mental condition and suffering of the terminally ill, much mental anguish associated with terminal illness simply goes beyond "treatable depression."

Critics of the terminal illness requirement point out that similar considerations may apply equally to persons who are likely to live with and suffer from debilitating diseases for years to come. If it would be compassionate to help a dying person avoid a final few days or weeks of suffering, it would be even more compassionate to accommodate a similar request from a person whose anticipated suffering must be measured in years.

The Argument from Autonomy

The second key value driving the argument for physician-assisted death is autonomy. In general, bioethicists are committed to the notion that competent individuals have the right to determine their own fates, particularly in personal matters of profound importance to them, so long as the rights of others are not violated in the process. The autonomy-based argument for physician-assisted death is straightforward: as illness begins to seriously compromise the quality of a person's life, few issues could be more profound and personal for that person than determining the point at which his or her life is no longer worth living. If adversity drains a person's life of meaning and transforms it into a burden, that person should have the right to determine when the time to die has come.

The right to refuse life-sustaining treatment is already firmly established. This demonstrates the depth of our respect for the value of autonomy in determining one's own "medical" fate, including the determination that "enough is enough." Those who favor physician-assisted death believe the scope of this right should be extended to include terminally ill patients who are not treatment-dependent.

Various critics of the terminal illness requirement have pointed out that, like the compassion rationale, the autonomy rationale for physician-assisted death also extends beyond the requirement of terminal illness. Nonterminal and terminal patients alike have the right to refuse life-sustaining treatment. If the underlying notion here is one of self-determination, the same logic seems to apply equally to terminal and nonterminal patients who have freely decided that their lives are no longer worth living.

The Argument from Fairness

The argument from fairness builds on the two previous arguments: since nonterminally ill patients may have equally compelling reasons for wanting to end their lives and an equal claim to self-determination, it would be arbitrary and hence unfair to restrict physician-assisted death to the terminally ill.

It is perhaps ironic that both advocates and critics of physician-assisted death can invoke these three arguments. Advocates can appeal to them for not limiting physician-assisted death to the terminally ill in the first place. At the same time, critics can point to them as attesting to the slipperiness of the public policy slope. They can claim that even if physician-assisted death is initially limited to those who are terminally ill, fairness will require that it be extended to others, and this would be disastrous.

The Argument from Vagueness

A fourth argument against the terminal illness requirement is that the concept of terminal illness is too vague and imprecise to do the regulatory job asked of it. In her concurrence in the 1997 Supreme Court decision on *Washington v. Glucksberg*, for instance, Justice Sandra O'Connor states that "the difficulty in defining terminal illness and the risk that a dying patient's request for assistance in ending his or her life might not be truly voluntary justifies the prohibitions on assisted suicide we uphold here."

The clearest and best-argued statement of this position is from Joanne Lynn and colleagues. They point out that physicians frequently underestimate or overestimate the survival rates of patients and often fail to acknowledge impending death until very close to the actual death. Moreover, attempts to define "terminal illness" more objectively (for example, in terms of a prognosis that specifies a certain likelihood of death within a certain time) will inevitably be over-inclusive or underinclusive: If the definition uses a low rate of survival (say, 20 percent survival rate in six months), then many patients will be declared not to be terminally ill who will in fact die within the relevant time period. On the other hand, if a high percentage is used (50 percent, for example), then many patients will be declared terminally ill who will live well beyond the relevant period. Citing data from the SUPPORT study [Study to Understand Prognoses and Preferences for Outcomes and Risks of Treatment], they argue convincingly that we will probably never be able to construct a definition of "terminal illness" that singles out all and only those who will die within a certain period.

Of course, whatever the definition of "terminal illness," any diagnosis of a particular patient as terminally ill will inevitably involve prediction and hence be subject to error. Even attempts to apply a definition that specifies a certain likelihood of death within a certain time will inevitably be misleading with respect to individual cases.

If the concept of terminal illness is so elusive as to be unintelligible, as Lynn and colleagues seem to suggest, that would certainly provide an insuperable objection to its use as a reasonable safeguard with respect to physician-assisted death—or in any other public policy consideration. This objection is thus fundamental to the case against the terminal illness requirement. The difficulty of defining "terminal illness" does not, however, generate a compelling reason for rejecting safeguards that rely on it.

An implicit premise of the argument from vagueness is that a definition of "terminal illness" is satisfactory only insofar as it singles out all and only those who will die within a precisely specified time. Behind this seems to lie the further assumption that physician-assisted death offers such marginal benefits and poses such grave risks that it would be irrational unless there were perfect safeguards. Critics argue in effect that attempts to restrict physician-assisted death to the terminally ill will not provide such a safeguard. We believe that both of these implicit premises are misguided.

In the first place, virtually no regulation, of any practice, is able to provide the sort of absolute assurance that Lynn seems to require for the terminal illness requirement. Statutes that provide for civil commitment, for example, often specify that the person must be suffering from a mental illness and present a danger to self or others. Clearly it is not possible to specify what constitutes a "danger" with great precision. It is not even possible to specify mental illness with great precision. In addition, the harm involved in mistakenly either committing or not committing someone is enormous. On the other hand, statutes that have great precision in their formulation also fail to provide total assurance of safety. A speed limit of 45 miles per hour for a given stretch of road is perfectly precise but fails to separate in all cases safe speeds from unsafe speeds. Sometimes weather conditions make travel at 45 miles per hour unsafe, while at other times the flow of traffic makes restricting oneself to 45 miles per hour unsafe.

Rather than requiring that safety regulations pick out target classes exactly, we often develop sets of regulations that, taken together, provide a high degree of safety without overly restricting worthy goals. The terminal illness requirement is no exception. The fact that it does not perfectly identify all and only those who are terminally ill does not mean that it lacks merit as a safeguard. It should be viewed as part of a package of regulations that also includes second opinions, age requirements, competency requirements, and so on. Clearly all of these contribute, albeit imperfectly, to ensure that those who opt for physician-assisted death do so only after making a fully autonomous, informed, and uncoerced choice.

Lynn and colleagues have noted a problem that is endemic to policies and regulations designed to promote imprecise goals. If we attempt to eliminate arbitrariness by drawing bright lines, we introduce arbitrariness when we pick the point to draw the line, knowing full well that some cases on each side of the line will fail to match our intentions. Alternatively, if we draft regulations with general language that reflects the general nature of the goal, we will not have sufficiently precise lines to avoid some arbitrary judgments about who falls within the scope of the regulation. The fact that no definition of "terminal illness" functions perfectly does not mean that it is not a reasonable safeguard. It is a safeguard, not a guarantee.

The Specialness of the Terminally Ill

The first three objections to the terminal illness requirement rely on the assumption that there is no morally relevant difference, at least as far as physician-assisted death is concerned, between those who are and those who are not terminally ill. The arguments based on compassion and autonomy indirectly assume that there is no morally relevant difference that can override the concerns of compassion or autonomy, and the argument from fairness infers from this that drawing a line at terminal illness is therefore morally arbitrary.

These arguments, however, focus exclusively on disputes about the potential benefits of allowing physician-assisted death. We agree that with respect to the potential benefits there are no morally relevant differences between terminally and nonterminally ill individuals who autonomously prefer death. Both terminally and nonterminally ill patients may experience intractable suffering so severe that access to physician-assisted death would be a genuine benefit. However, we believe that with respect to risks there may be important differences between terminally ill patients and others.

There is no rock-solid empirical evidence regarding the dangers of physician-assisted death for either terminally ill patients or others. Nonetheless, we believe there is some fairly compelling evidence, to be found in current treatment practices for terminally ill patients, which suggests that allowing them access to physician-assisted death would involve negligible additional risk. In contrast, there is no comparable assurance for patients who are not terminally ill. This clearly represents a morally relevant difference. In light of this difference—especially given that current opposition to physician-assisted death is grounded largely on concern about potential risks—it is reasonable to begin by allowing terminally ill patients access to physician-assisted death and awaiting better evidence about the dangers of physician-assisted death and the effectiveness of the safeguards before deciding whether to make physician-assisted death available to those who are not terminally ill, adhere to the terminal illness requirement, or retreat to a complete ban on physician-assisted death.

A Difference in Risks

In treating terminally ill patients, we already permit medical techniques that hasten death and have the same potential for unjustifiable deaths as physician-assisted death. The right to refuse even life-sustaining treatment is currently beyond legal dispute. Other, even more significant medical practices involve attempts to control pain that can actually hasten death. Perhaps the most common of these is the practice of providing painkilling narcotics at doses sufficient to relieve pain while clearly foreseeing that the narcotics may well suppress respiration. "Double-effect deaths" can result from the suppressed respiration. "Terminal sedation," a more controversial practice, involves placing a terminally ill person in a medically induced coma and allowing the patient to die from starvation and dehydration.

Theoretically, either of these practices could be provided to nonterminally ill patients complaining of unbearable suffering. In practice, however, many physicians are reluctant to provide terminal sedation even for terminally ill patients. A suffering nonterminally ill patient would currently find it extremely difficult to locate a health care provider willing to give such sedation knowing it would facilitate death (and arguably suicide).

Clearly, all of the arguments about the risks of mistakes or abuse in implementing physician-assisted death could also be directed against these other practices, including even simple withholding or withdrawal of life-prolonging therapies. In fact, however, they seldom are, and they certainly do not prompt us to ban those practices. On the contrary, the recent emphasis on improving palliative care of the dying has emphasized the importance of being willing to risk double effect deaths in order to manage pain adequately.

Our society's experience with hospice—also limited to terminally ill patients—also suggests that the risks of physician-assisted death may be acceptable. At the core of hospice philosophy is a commitment to the notion that at some point, terminally ill patients are ill served by coercive expectations to submit to intrusive and often painful life-prolonging therapies. Hospice offers the option of dying in an environment that is supportive of the decision to forgo such treatments and to receive only optimal palliative care to ease one's passing. Today most Americans die following some termination-of-treatment decision. The effort to persuade people to draw up advance directives is a proper attempt to ensure that these decisions are the patients' as much as possible.

No one still argues that the risks of coercion and duress justify prohibiting terminally ill patients from electing to forgo life-prolonging treatment by entering hospice. Today it is generally recognized that such a choice is completely understandable and reasonable, and one that should be supported. Advocates believe that for the same reason, terminally ill patients should be allowed access to physician-assisted death. As several authors have argued in detail, there is no more reason to suppose that they would be coerced than that those who refuse life-prolonging therapies or enter hospice programs would be coerced.

In fact, we see reason to suppose that the practices we've just described may involve a greater risk of coercion than the proposed practice of allowing physicians to grant terminally ill patients' requests for prescriptions that can be used to end their lives. Alan Meisel has recently pointed out that even the practice of terminating life-sustaining treatment may be more dangerous than physician-assisted suicide, since such decisions routinely must be made for persons who are unconscious or incompetent, while physician-assisted suicide requires the autonomous action of the patient, not merely of a proxy. This point applies as well to the decision to risk a double effect death in order to provide adequate pain relief, since these patients are likely to be incompetent. The decision to enter a hospice program is made jointly by patient and physician and, once made, sets institutional wheels in motion involving the hospice, the hospital, and possibly third-party payers. The role of other parties could prove troublesome and coercive for the patient who has last-minute second thoughts about "giving up hope" on life-prolonging therapies. Deciding at the last minute not to go into hospice could be perceived by the patient and doctor as an instance of patient noncompliance. By contrast, the final decision to take life-ending medications to which a physician has provided access is the patient's alone—and if the patient does not take the medications, any decent physician would be pleased. It may be that the restoration of control achieved by providing the medication had also restored an acceptable quality of life. Thus if critics are correct that physicians can exercise undue influence on the patient, the problem would seem to count more against allowing terminally ill patients to elect to enter hospice than it does against physician-assisted death.

There is another reason to suppose that terminally ill persons are less likely to incur risks than those who are not terminally ill. Terminally ill patients are, after all, dying. They cannot decide whether to die in the near future. At best they can only decide how they will die. As many of them come to grips with this fact and as they see control of both their bodies and their lives slipping away, the question of when and how they will die can understandably become a central and reasonable concern. Such persons may reasonably give high priority to dying well. Indeed this goal, coupled with determination, may be of significant meaning for the dying person. For these people, the option of physician-assisted death can provide great benefit, since it restores a key measure of control over their situation. The mere fact of having control restored (either by obtaining the necessary drugs or by knowing that they are available) can for some terminally ill patients transform an unendurable existence into one in which the patient can again find enough meaning and value that she never actually takes the lethal medications. One study, for instance, indicated that only 59 percent of terminally ill patients to whom a physician gave a lethal prescription used the drug to commit suicide.

Of course, as the criticisms from compassion and autonomy point out, some nonterminally ill patients might also gain comparable benefits if physician-assisted death were available to them. And conversely, there's always a risk that some terminally ill patients might elect physician-assisted death unwisely, safeguards notwithstanding. However, terminally ill patients as a group are less at risk for unwise decisions, since so many of them are already coming to terms with dying for reasons we can understand. Put differently, there is a much greater likelihood that a nonterminal patient who wishes to die could be restored to a meaningful existence, and hence a much greater chance that physician-assisted death would be a mistake for that patient, than would be the case for a patient near death and for whom the time and the manner of death now loom as the only remaining central questions of their lives.

An Incremental Approach

We believe physician-assisted death should be made available to terminally ill patients. The affirmative arguments based on compassion and autonomy are compelling and the prevailing risk-based objections to physician-assisted death for terminally ill patients can be rebutted. Legalizing and thereby regulating physician-assisted death does not put terminally ill patients at greater risk than do other, already accepted practices in the treatment of the terminally ill.

With respect to nonterminal patients, however, the situation is otherwise. Opponents argue vigorously that legalization of physician-assisted death would expose vulnerable populations—persons with disabilities, the poor, and socially stigmatized groups—to a new and intolerable risk. Others, ourselves included, believe these fears are exaggerated, and that ultimately even vulnerable persons would be better served by expanding their legal rights to determine their own ultimate fates than by paternalistically protecting them from the risk of making unwise decisions.

In light of the current paucity of evidence, however, it is reasonable to proceed incrementally and extend physician-assisted death initially only to terminally ill patients. Doing so will grant its benefits to those who as a group are most likely to benefit and for whom it would involve no more risk than do current medical practices at the end of life, while withholding it from those less apt to benefit and about whom there is greater controversy over potential risk. Finally, opting for the incremental approach will generate further data that can subsequently make possible a more reasonable assessment of the risk.

Currently such risk assessments are highly speculative. While some data is available, at present the empirical evidence supporting claims that physician-assisted death poses significant risks is sketchy at best. Even some who insist that physician-assisted death is too risky decry the paucity of evidence. Ezekiel Emanuel, for instance, states that "it is impossible to overemphasize the tenuous nature of our ability to predict what will happen if [physician-assisted suicide] or euthanasia is legalized," and concludes that "regrettably, the data do not permit any quantitative assessment of harms."

Thus the restriction of physician-assisted death to terminally ill patients should not necessarily be regarded as a permanent restriction. Our defense of the terminal illness requirement is based not on deep principle, but rather on risk assessment in the face of uncertainty. If physician-assisted death were extended to terminally ill patients, we could decide to stop there, retreat, or advance, depending on what we found out.

Legalization of Euthanasia in the Netherlands Is Dangerous

Christianity Today

This selection describes what the editors of *Christianity Today* regard as an alarming development: the legalization of euthanasia and physician-assisted suicide in the Netherlands by a bill passed by the lower house of the Dutch Parliament. Previously, the editors explain, these acts were technically illegal, although doctors who carried them out were almost never punished. The editors describe different countries' reactions to the legislation, which, they say, makes the Netherlands the first country in the world to legalize euthanasia and physician-assisted suicide. *Christianity Today* is published weekly by Christianity Today Inc., which was founded by Billy Graham.

Few seem to have noticed the euthanasia movement's latest gains.

In the last week of November 2000, the lower house of the Dutch Parliament passed a bill that made the Netherlands the first country in the world to legalize euthanasia and physician-assisted suicide (PAS). U.S. newspapers printed brief wire stories about the event, but our nation's editorialists and opinion writers were distracted by the contested U.S. presidential election.

In the first week of December, *The New England Journal of Medicine* published a report by four medical researchers, showing that 75 percent of those who had died at the hands of Jack Kevorkian, Michigan's grandstanding advocate of PAS, were not actually terminally ill. Again the nation's newspapers printed only well-buried wire stories.

Unfortunately, the media focus on the Florida presidential ballot recount, as important as it was, failed to keep us informed on developments with serious moral consequences; and it missed an opportunity to stimulate public debate on a vital public concern.

The Netherlands Legalizes Euthanasia

Here is some of what American readers missed:

1. The lower house of the Dutch Parliament passed a more restrictive bill than euthanasia and PAS advocates had been

pushing for. Originally, the bill would have extended the age for euthanasia without parental consent as low as 12 years. Fortunately, this proposal of the radical D66 party was unable to garner a majority. But the new law still accords this level of autonomy to 16-year-olds.

2. The parliamentary vote was lopsided. The bill passed 104-40, reflecting the attitudes of the Dutch population, which some reports pegged at 90 percent in favor. Only the Christian Democrats and three small Calvinist parties voted against the bill. The upper house's approval of the bill in spring 2001 is expected to be a mere formality.

3. In Canada and the United Kingdom, PAS activists quickly used the event as a platform for renewed advocacy, but the German reaction was swift and negative. According to a United Press International (UPI) report, a spokesman for the Marburger Bund, a powerful association of hospital physicians, said, "Killing does not belong to the duties of a doctor." And Hartmut Steeb, secretary-general of Germany's Evangelical Alliance, said, "This law shows that the lessons from the human rights catastrophe in the Third Reich have not been learned."

In Germany, the moral memory of Aktion T4, Hitler's euthanasia law, is still alive. But the Dutch seem to have forgotten that Hitler's regime first sharpened its execution skills and tested its gas chambers on sick children and disabled adults from 1939 to 1941 before it applied its new technical expertise to Jews at Auschwitz and Treblinka.

4. The Dutch law still considers euthanasia and assisted suicide as crimes—unless it is performed by a doctor and under certain clearly spelled-out conditions. Advocates claim those conditions will help prevent abuse.

But for more than two decades, euthanasia and PAS have been tolerated by the Dutch courts within certain guidelines—and those guidelines have been regularly flouted. According to a 1999 study cited by Canada's *National Post,* of all the Dutch cases of euthanasia and PAS in 1995, 20 percent of the deaths took place without the patient's express consent, 56 percent were not motivated by "unbearable suffering" but by "loss of dignity," and nearly two-thirds were not reported to authorities as required.

Advocates of the new law, such as D66 leader Thom DeGraaf, say the new measures are "for people who are in great pain and have no prospect for recovery." But the widespread practice of ignoring the existing guidelines suggests, as Bert Dorenbos of Cry for Life has said, that such laws only amount to issuing the medical profession a license to kill.

5. Terminal illness is only a minor factor among those who seek PAS or euthanasia. Historian Kevin Yuill reported in *The Specta-*

tor that in Holland "only 2 or 3 percent of all patients with terminal illnesses choose voluntary euthanasia." In the study of
Kevorkian's "patients," only 25 percent appeared to be terminally ill, according to autopsy findings. The number of those
who had experienced recent decline in health status, and who
therefore may have been seriously discouraged, was 72 percent.
And a large percentage were experiencing some sort of social isolation. The divorced, widowed, and never-married were disproportionately represented at 69 percent. In addition, a *Detroit Free
Press* study of three "patients" who had "no medical problems"
found that all "took mood-altering drugs and painkillers, and
had histories of psychiatric problems or diseases that were difficult to diagnose."

The role of discouragement, depression, and social isolation
in death decisions must be studied very carefully, for the experience of isolation can mesh with the cultural values of individu-
alism in dangerous ways.

One Canadian pundit wrote that "if the Netherlands didn't
exist, high school debating clubs would have to invent it" and
called the country "a one-stop shop for libertarian ideas." Those
libertarian ideas—which include a broad tolerance of drugs,
sex-for-sale, and gay marriage—are descended from a noble
Dutch tradition of individual freedom. After the Reformation,
English pilgrims and Swiss Anabaptists found a haven from religious persecution in Holland before eventually migrating to
American shores. Today's Dutch libertarianism is a perversion
of that fine tradition.

The libertarian arguments offered by euthanasia and PAS
advocates appeal to highly individualized notions of autonomy,
rationality, and dignity. But the best biblical and secular thinkers
have recognized that we are inescapably social creatures, and
that we are most free when we are enmeshed in supportive, intimate relationships. Living or dying, it is not good for man to be
alone. Divorced from emotional and physical support systems,
an individual can easily rationalize the urge to end life. However, in the context of mutual support, enormous suffering can
be borne and transcended for the sake of love.

Stewardship of Lives

6. The argument is becoming increasingly centered on belief in
God. Yes, much liberal Christian rhetoric appeals to so-called
compassion. And the Hemlock Society is not ignoring the super-
natural dimension. (It even has "chaplains" who help candi-
dates weigh their choices in the light of the suspect literature on
Near Death Experiences.)

But arguments against euthanasia or PAS fail to persuade

when they are divorced from belief in God. Writing in Canada's *National Post,* an advocate of PAS who is unconvinced by mushy religious arguments called for clarity:

> Arguing about the risk of abuse in the context of euthanasia is a lot like weighing the evidence of crime deterrence in the context of capital punishment: It is merely a rhetorical sideshow in which pundits who have already decided the issue along ideological and spiritual lines trot out empirical studies that happen to support their side. The Vatican denounces the new Dutch bill as an affront to "human dignity." [Bioethicist Margaret] Somerville tells us euthanasia does violence to "the human spirit" and our "sense of the sacred." At their root, both arguments represent variations on the same mystical idea: that it is somehow degrading and morally wrong if the time and manner of a human death is not left to a higher power. Only by invoking God . . . can opponents of euthanasia overcome the utilitarian presumption that it is correct and good to answer a person's plea for death.

That quote is an ideological and "rhetorical sideshow" in its own right. Nevertheless, it inadvertently makes the same point that the Canadian newspaper *Christian Week* made less colorfully: Secular ethics has hit a dead end. Shun utilitarian thinking. Only revealed ethics can address this issue safely.

What are we to make of this challenge? We are not our own. We belong to each other and to God, both by creation and redemption. We are bought with a price, to use St. Paul's words. Life is thus for us a matter of stewardship rather than ownership. And the lives entrusted to us are to be loved and nurtured until the Master takes them from us.

Moves to Block Oregon Law

7. The battle continues in the United States. In Oregon, where PAS has been legalized, a fundraising letter for the Compassion in Dying Federation declares, "We have expanded our mission to include not only terminally ill individuals, but also persons with incurable illnesses which will eventually lead to a terminal diagnosis." That definition, the *National Post* editorial page points out, "covers myriad conditions, including early-stage cancer and heart disease." The federation's director of legal affairs even claims that Oregon's 15-day waiting period is "overly restrictive" and "unduly burdensome."

   In the Senate, Majority Whip Don Nickles (R-Okla.) has sponsored the Pain Relief Promotion Act. This bill, which was backed by the American Medical Association, would protect and promote the appropriate use of pain medication, but it would also bar physicians from using federally controlled substances to aid a suicide. In effect, it would encourage physicians to prescribe generously for pain, while it would also void Oregon's maverick PAS law. In an unforeseen upset in December 2000, liberal senators won a public-relations campaign and defeated Nickles's efforts to attach his provisions to the final spending bill of 2000.

Ron Wyden (D-Oreg.) said he expects President Bush to instruct his new attorney general to reinterpret the Controlled Substances Act to invalidate the Oregon law. For his part, Bush has said he would sign a version of the Nickles bill. Let us hope he does both. But ultimately, it is up to all who see themselves as stewards of a divine gift to model their belief in compassionate care for the dying and the discouraged.

CHAPTER 4

EUTHANASIA IN
PRACTICE

OREGON'S FIRST REPORT LEAVES MANY QUESTIONS UNANSWERED

Kathleen Foley and Herbert Hendin

Kathleen Foley and Herbert Hendin, two opponents of physician-assisted suicide, claim that the Oregon Health Department's report on the assisted suicides carried out during the first year of the state's Death with Dignity Act (1998) leaves out important information. For example, Foley and Hendin write, the report contains no accounts from patients or their families. Foley is a professor of neurology, neuroscience, and clinical pharmacology at Cornell University Medical College. Hendin is a professor of psychiatry at New York Medical College and medical director of the American Foundation for Suicide Prevention.

In a public document, an article in the *New England Journal of Medicine*, a National Press Club briefing, and visits to various congressional offices, the Oregon Health Division (OHD) argued in early 1999 that assisted suicide is being carried out safely under the state's Death with Dignity Act. Unfortunately, the report is marked by its failure to address the limits of the information it has available, overreaching its data to draw unwarranted conclusions. Most striking, and least justified, is its contention without substantiating patient data that patients who were assisted in suicide were receiving adequate end-of-life care. In fact, we know nothing about the physical, psychological, and existential needs of the patients requesting assisted suicide. We know little of the capabilities of the physicians who are responding to those requests. And we know nothing of the context in which these patients live and are cared for.

We opposed the legislation, but since it was passed both advocates and opponents share a responsibility to see to it that the law is administered so as to best protect patients. If insufficient data is being obtained in a flawed monitoring process, everyone should be concerned.

Limited Data

The data OHD has collected is largely epidemiological: the assisted suicide cases were divided between men and women, the median age

From "The Oregon Report: Don't Ask, Don't Tell," by Kathleen Foley and Herbert Hendin, *The Hastings Center Report*, May 1999. Copyright © 1999 Hastings Center. Used with permission.

of the patients was sixty-nine, all the patients were white, all but two of them had cancer, and the patients who chose assisted suicide were more likely to be divorced or never to have married. Physicians participating in assisted suicide are not asked to provide OHD with significant medical information about their patients. They are merely asked to check off a list on an OHD form indicating that such statutory requirements as a written request for a lethal dose of medication, a fifteen-day waiting period, and consultation with another physician have been met. Only one line is provided for both diagnosis and prognosis, although a diagnosis of terminal illness and prognosis of death within six months are the essential requirements for assisted suicide in the state. The form does not inquire on what basis the physician made the medical diagnosis—for example, review of x-rays, written material, pathology reports, or other information. Nor are physicians asked to report on what basis they made the prognosis—what tables they have used, what experts they have consulted. The form does not even inquire as to the patient's reasons for requesting assisted suicide. The data do not make it possible to know what transpired in any particular case.

To supplement the meager information required by formal reporting, OHD asked physicians who participated in assisted suicide to respond in person or by phone to a questionnaire that was also given to physicians of a comparison (control) group of patients who died of similar illnesses without assisted suicide. OHD does not tell us who asked the questions, what their training was, and whether any follow-up questions were asked. But the questionnaire (published on the Internet) and the report show that this effort was also flawed. Missing medical information was not asked for or provided.

In the absence of medical data, how does OHD reach its conclusion that patients received adequate end-of-life care? From the facts—derived from the physician questionnaire—that the proportion of patients who had advance directives and were enrolled in hospice programs was comparably high for both the case and comparison groups, and that neither worry about pain control nor financial concerns drove patients' requests for assisted suicide. But neither advance directives nor enrollment in a hospice program provides proof of competent assessment and treatment—the essential components of adequate care—any more than does patients' apparent silence about palliative care or financial concerns. Such figures cannot substitute for direct knowledge of patients and their illnesses. Although the physicians questioned reported that more patients requesting assisted suicide were concerned with loss of autonomy or loss of control of body functions than were those in the control group, physicians were not asked how these concerns were expressed or addressed. Without such information it is not possible to judge the adequacy of the care these patients received.

Palliative Care

Under the Oregon law, when a terminally ill patient requests assisted suicide, physicians are required to point out that palliative care and hospice care are feasible alternatives. They are not required, however, to be knowledgeable about how to relieve either physical or emotional suffering in terminally ill patients. Without such knowledge, and without inquiry into why the patient requested assisted suicide, the physician cannot present feasible alternatives. Serious evaluation of the end-of-life care that such patients received would have to be conducted by physicians trained in palliative care, able and willing to inquire about the nature of the patient's illness and concerns and what was done to address them. We do not know that those at OHD administering the questionnaire had such training.

The report stresses the fact that only one of the fifteen patients expressed concern about inadequate pain control at the end of life. The report's authors believe this may reflect advances in palliative care in Oregon and the fact that the state ranks high in the use of morphine for medical purposes. Yet fifteen of the forty-three control patients were worried about end-of-life pain control, suggesting the concern is frequent among those who are terminally ill. But the figures themselves are suspect. They are based on physicians' responses long after the fact to the question whether patients volunteered such concerns about pain. The physicians did not directly ask the patients about their pain. The inadequacy of relying on physicians' perceptions of patients' experiences has long been documented, particularly with regard to pain: in numerous published studies physicians underestimated what patients were experiencing. In surveys of barriers to effective pain relief, patients reported that they did not want to use their time with their doctors to discuss pain relief but rather to discuss their treatments. This is particularly apt to be true of patients requesting assisted suicide, who if successful in persuading physicians to give them a lethal prescription would have no need to be concerned about future pain. A study surveying cancer patients with pain or depression showed how differences in their attitudes toward physician-assisted suicide would affect their choice of physicians: Patients with pain reported they would change physicians if they knew their physician participated in physician-assisted suicide. Those with depression were more likely to seek out such physicians.

Surveys of family members of dying patients can provide insight into the adequacy of palliative care services. The OHD report fails to cite the recent Oregon Board of Medical Examiners (BME) survey of 475 surviving family members listed as informants from a stratified sample of Oregon death certificates for 1997; the survey showed a statewide trend of higher rates of moderate to severe pain reported by family members of patients dying in acute care hospitals throughout Oregon. The BME viewed the trend as a "worrisome" statistic that suggested inadequate palliative care.

No data are available in the Oregon report on the major symptoms other than pain that interfere with patient quality of life and affect their sense of autonomy and control.

The report, however, does help settle one medical debate that went on between advocates and opponents prior to implementation of the law. Opponents of legalizing assisted suicide in Oregon pointed out that because there was no reliable information about the lethal dose of drugs for medically ill patients, physicians assisting suicide would essentially be experimenting on patients. In Dutch studies 20 percent of patients given 9 grams of barbiturates, considered a lethal dose, lived for more than three hours. Dutch doctors usually then intervened with a lethal injection, which would be illegal in Oregon. In a number of reported cases in this country, after swallowing presumed lethal doses of barbiturates patients did not die and families intervened with pillows or plastic bags. Advocacy groups denied the validity of the Dutch findings and of such accounts although recommending the 9-gram barbiturate dose, which was given by Oregon physicians to fourteen of the fifteen Oregon cases. OHD notes without comment that four of the fifteen patients lived longer than three hours and one lived as long as eleven—figures that are consistent with the Dutch experience.

Economic Factors

The pitfalls that result from OHD's inadequate methodology are nowhere more apparent than in its conclusion that economic factors did not influence the choice of assisted suicide. OHD informs us that apprehensions that assisted suicide would be chosen by those "fearful of the financial consequences of their illness" were unjustified. This may or may not be true, but the OHD is not in a position to know. The Oregon law does not ask physicians to inquire about patients' economic or social circumstances, nor does OHD require physicians to report such information.

On the basis of the physician questionnaire OHD concludes, "None of the case patients or control patients expressed concern to their physicians about the financial impact of their illness. We found no significant difference between the case patients and the control patients with regard to insurance at the time of their death."

The apparent lack of differences between the case and control groups is more likely to reflect the lack of sensitivity of the model and the superficiality of the data collected. It is very unusual for physicians to have a clear understanding of the financial issues facing their patients. More commonly they are unaware of patients' out-of-pocket expenses, or of other family and personal considerations. Physicians have little time to discuss these issues and patients have strong needs (out of pride) not to provide this information to clinicians. A patient requesting assisted suicide may also feel that the request is less likely to be granted if the physician feels that the patient is making the request because he or she cannot afford proper care. Yet certainly when a patient requests assisted suicide one would expect physicians to inquire about the patient's ability to afford adequate care, whether or not the patient raises the question and even though the law does not suggest that physicians do so.

Even among the insured there is compelling evidence to suggest that the cost of end-of-life care can contribute to financial hardship. In a comprehensive study of end-of-life care, more than half of the families involved in the care of a seriously ill family member reported at least one severe financial burden, ranging from loss of family savings and loss of income to changes in future educational plans or employment status. High deductibles, copayments or a coinsurance, and limits of coverage can all contribute to high out-of-pocket expenditures. Medicare covers only 83 percent of typical charges for lung cancer and 65 percent of typical charges for breast cancer; it does not reimburse for out-of-pocket drug expenses, which can be particularly burdensome. And hospice provides only limited nursing care (four hours per day) unless the patient is imminently dying.

Evaluation for Depression

Since Oregon is the first state to legalize suicide as a treatment for medical illness, it would seem to have a special responsibility to protect the significant numbers of patients who become suicidally depressed in response to serious or terminal illness. We know that medical illness is an important factor in 70 percent of all suicides over the age of sixty. We know also that two-thirds of all suicides and two-thirds of those requesting physician-assisted suicide are suffering from depression. Among patients requesting assisted suicide researchers have found depression to be the only factor that significantly predicts the wish for death.

Although a psychiatric evaluation is the standard of care for suicidal patients, the Oregon law does not require it in assisted suicide cases. Under the law, only if the physician believes that the patient might be suffering from a psychiatric or psychological disorder or from a depression causing impaired judgment must the physician refer the patient to a licensed psychiatrist or psychologist for counseling. Yet studies have shown that physicians are not reliably able to diagnose depression, let alone to determine whether the depression is impairing judgment. Passik noted in a study of cancer patients with moderate to severe depression that only 13 percent of clinicians identified depression in the patient population. With such facts in mind, a task force organized by the Oregon Health Sciences University to guide caregivers advised physicians to refer all cases requesting assisted suicide for psychiatric evaluation even though they are not legally required to do so.

Does OHD monitor the process to see to it that depressed patients are adequately protected? Psychiatrists who have examined patients and found them depressed, with "impaired judgment," are not even asked to file a report with OHD. Buried in a table but not discussed in the report is the fact that only four of the fifteen patients who requested assistance in suicide were referred for psychiatric or psychological evaluation. Since all fifteen cases went forward we must conclude that in no case was depression or any other mental illness considered to be compromising the patient's judgment.

If OHD wished to monitor the psychiatric evaluation, a trained psychiatrist or psychologist should have interviewed both the prescribing physicians and the psychiatrists who saw the four patients who were evaluated. Questions such as those asked in a psychological autopsy would be asked: Were the reasons for requesting assisted suicide explored? How did the physician evaluate them? What was the physician's response? Was the patient depressed? What were the symptoms? Was treatment offered? What was the patient's response? What other risk factors for suicide were present, such as a family history of depression and/or suicide, alcoholism, or any past suicide attempts? What was the patient's past experience with the death of those close to him or her? Did the patient—like most suicides and assisted suicides—express any ambivalence about suicide? If so how was this expressed and how was it dealt with? Physicians inexperienced in dealing with suicidal patients tend to take requests to die literally and concretely, failing to hear this ambivalence.

It would have been valuable to compare interviews with physicians of eight additional patients who requested but did not carry out assisted suicide: six who died of their underlying illnesses without using lethal prescriptions given them and two who were still alive on 1 January 1999. This information was not obtained. Yet at least the first six are essentially dropouts in the study, a group that investigators normally wish to compare with their cases. Such patients might provide us with further insights into the complicated aspects of patient requests.

OHD might well consider that psychiatric assessment is intended under the Oregon law to deal only with the limited issue of a patient's capacity to make the decision for assisted suicide. But then at a minimum OHD would need to monitor on what basis clinicians referred patients for psychiatric evaluation and whether these decisions were appropriate. The psychiatrists approving the assisted suicide would have to be interviewed to learn how well they knew the patient, whether the patient was seen more than once, and on what basis they decided the patient was competent. When surveyed, only 6 percent of Oregon psychiatrists were confident that absent a long-term relationship with a patient they could satisfactorily determine in a single visit whether that patient was competent to commit suicide. The same survey revealed that the majority of those willing to evaluate a patient's competence for assisted suicide favor the practice, leading the investigators to conclude that "a bias may be introduced into the competency evaluation." When advocacy groups, like Compassion in Dying, are shepherding the cases and the referrals, the likelihood of such bias would seem to be even greater.

A Public Case

Although the Oregon report tells us nothing about any individual case, we do know a little about one of the fifteen patients who requested and carried out assisted suicide. The first case known to the public under the new law was publicized by Compassion in Dying, the advocacy group shepherding many of the Oregon assisted suicides.

The patient was described as being in her mid-80s with metastatic breast cancer and in a hospice program. The patient's own physician had not been willing to assist in her suicide for reasons that were not specified. A second physician also refused on the grounds that she was depressed. Her husband called Compassion in Dying and was referred to a doctor willing to participate. The doctor referred the patient to a second physician and to a psychiatrist who supported the decision. Much of the information about the case came from an audiotape the physician made of an interview he had with the patient. An edited version of the audiotape was played for the media by Compassion in Dying the day after the patient's death.

On the tape, said to have been made two days before she died, the patient says of her impending death "I'm looking forward to it. . . . I will be relieved of all the stress I have."

The patient expressed concern about her autonomy, specifically about being artificially fed, a concern that suggests some vulnerability and uncertainty about her course of action. The physician does not assure her that this need not happen in any case. He ignores the remark and instead asks a question designed to elicit a response about her desire to die.

> Patient: I've seen people suffer, they give them artificial feeding and stuff, which is really not doing anything for them in the long run.
>
> Doctor: Can you explain how you feel about dying in a few days?

There is no indication that this physician was trying to find any feasible alternatives to suicide. In the taped interview released to the public the physician follows the law's requirement, simply listing other choices she could make: hospice support, chemotherapy, and hormonal therapy.

Doctor: There is, of course, all sorts of hospice support that is available to you. There is, of course, chemotherapy that is available that may or may not have any effect, not in curing your cancer, but perhaps in lengthening your life to some extent. And there is also available a hormone which you were offered before by the oncologist—tamoxifen—which is not really chemotherapy but would have some possibility of slowing or stopping the course of the disease for some period of time.

Patient: Yes, I don't want to take that.

Doctor: All right, OK, that's pretty much what you need to understand.

The case raises disturbing questions. The physicians who evaluated the patient offered two contradictory sets of opinions about the appropriateness of her decision. As the decisionmaking process progressed, it provided no mechanism for resolving the disagreement based on medical expertise, such as that which can be provided by an ethics committee that would hear the facts of the case before going forward. Instead, the opinions of the two doctors who did not support the patient's decision—one of whom knew her for some time and the other who considered that she was depressed—are essentially ignored.

To evaluate fairly the adequacy of the end-of-life care provided this patient OHD would need to interview her first two physicians as well as those who participated in the assisted suicide. The report indicates that in six of the fifteen cases the first physician seen by the patient did not agree to assist in the suicide; none of these physicians were contacted by OHD. And although the OHD reported that none of the cases in either the case group or the control group expressed financial concerns, a member of this patient's family told a reporter for *The Oregonian* that the patient was concerned that her financial resources not be dissipated by her care.

Avoiding Hard Questions

The flaws in OHD's monitoring come in part from the problems and flaws in the Oregon law. Intolerable and unrelievable suffering—a requirement for assisted suicide in the Netherlands—is not a requirement of the Oregon law; the diagnosis of a terminal illness is sufficient. The presumption and stipulation in the Oregon law that a diagnosis of terminal illness is sufficient for assisted suicide does not encourage physicians to inquire into the source of the medical, psychological, social, and existential concerns that usually underlie such a request, an inquiry that leads patients and physicians to have the kind of discussion that often leads to relief for patients and makes assisted suicide seem unnecessary. Nor are physicians asked or required by the

Oregon law to make such an inquiry. Certainly such a discussion with the patient described above would have included consideration of her fears of being artificially fed and assurance that she did not need to choose assisted suicide in order for that not to happen.

Although the questionnaire given to physicians provides three lines for them to reply to a question as to why their patients chose to request assisted suicide, if the physicians had not previously explored the matter with their patients those replies are of questionable value. That the Oregon Health Sciences University which examined the law felt it necessary to recommend that physicians ask patients why they are requesting assisted suicide suggests this weakness of the law, how unprepared Oregon physicians are to deal with it, and how unprotected Oregon patients are by it.

OHD monitoring reflects the law's predilections so that OHD seems determined not to ask the tough questions and not to ask them of the right people. Patients are not asked to complete and provide any information to the state. Over 70 percent of the patients were in hospice care but, since OHD did not interview hospice staff, hospice nurses and social workers who may have the most knowledge of the patients were given no voice in the monitoring process. And the information physicians provide is far too limited to be relevant to those wanting to understand the end-of-life care these patients receive.

The physicians who did not agree to assist in suicide are not interviewed by the OHD and on the basis of doctor-patient confidentiality cannot speak publicly about the reasons for their refusal. This is in contrast to physician advocates, some of whom talk and write publicly about the treatment. One wonders if they have their patients' permission to do so.

Neutral Observers or Advocates?

Fifteen cases in a year was seen as a small number and as such interpreted as indicating that the law was not likely to be abused. In such a controversial procedure, however, one might expect patients and physicians to be at first hesitant about participating. Although we do not have figures for the early years in the Netherlands when assisted suicide and euthanasia were first given legal sanction, they appear to have been practiced at first relatively infrequently. It was only after the practice became generally accepted for some years that the numbers rose significantly. Some of the early Dutch patients were advocates of assisted suicide who used their deaths partly to make a statement in behalf of a cause in which they believed. There has been some question as to whether the Oregon patients might either be advocates or disproportionately shepherded by advocacy groups to chosen physicians. The physician questionnaire partly addressed this latter concern in asking, "Was the patient specifically referred to you regarding PAS by an organization such as Compassion in Dying or the Hemlock Society?" Inexplicably, OHD did not publish the answer. We know, however, from the period when those organizations thought it useful to publicize their involvement, that the first few patients were referred through them to physicians who would prescribe lethal medication.

After information about the first case had been made public, one of the authors of the OHD report told *The Oregonian* that too much information had been revealed. "They [the public] want to know [the law] worked in general and other than that they were almost embarrassed to read about the details." She went on to say that it would seldom happen in the future. If what we know about the first assisted suicide is at all true of others, details about how the law is operating would probably be more embarrassing to OHD than to the public.

What is perhaps most disturbing in Oregon—and most similar to the Netherlands—is that those administering the law and those sanctioned by the government to analyze its operation have become its advocates. The overreaching conclusions in the OHD report and the public relations campaign that accompanied its release—from the National Press Club briefing to the visits to various Congressional offices—seem to belie the claim of its authors that they are simply a "neutral party" collecting data.

OHD has a higher responsibility, to present what it knows and admit what it does not. The ideal solution would be for OHD to appoint a task force made up of physicians from out of the state who are experts in palliative care, psychiatry, and medicine to review the assisted suicide cases. Perhaps even to embark on a prospective study. Unless physicians are asked to report more than they are now required to under the law, and unless properly trained independent physicians can question the physicians and examine the data, we will not learn much from the Oregon experience. Nor will we be assured that patients who choose assisted suicide are receiving appropriate care at the end of life.

Report on Oregon's Third Year of Legalized Physician-Assisted Suicide

Oregon Health Division

This report from the Oregon Health Division provides information about the 26 terminally ill people who killed themselves in the year 2000 by means of prescriptions obtained under the state's Death with Dignity Act. The report compares these people with those who took advantage of the law in 1998 and 1999. It also discusses the reasons that the people gave for wanting assistance in dying. The Health Division is part of the Oregon Department of Human Services.

After voters reaffirmed the Death with Dignity Act (DWDA) in 1997, Oregon became the only state allowing legal physician-assisted suicide (PAS). Mandated reporting of prescriptions for lethal medication provides the Oregon Health Division (OHD) with a unique opportunity to describe terminally ill patients choosing legal PAS. During 1998 and 1999, 16 and 27 patients, respectively, used PAS. In these first two years we looked at demographic factors—such as age, sex, race, marital status, education, and residence in the Portland metro area—and reasons why patients choose to request a prescription for lethal medication. Demographically, patients using PAS were better educated than other Oregonians dying of similar diseases. Physician and family members indicated that patient requests for lethal medications stemmed from multiple concerns related to autonomy and control at the end of life.

This report reviews the monitoring and data collection system that was implemented under the law, and summarizes the information collected on patients and physicians who participated in the Act in its third year of implementation (January 1, 2000 to December 31, 2000). Using physician reports and interviews, and death certificates, we address the following three questions: Are numbers of patients using legal PAS in Oregon increasing? Do patients who participated in 2000 demographically resemble patients using PAS in previous years and other Oregonians dying from similar diseases? Do physician reports

From "Oregon's Death with Dignity Act: Three Years of Legalized Physician-Assisted Suicide," by the Oregon Health Division, Oregon Department of Human Services, Health Division, available at www.ohd.hr.state.or.us/chs/pas/ar-about.htm. Used with permission.

indicate differences in patients' motivations for using PAS over the past three years?

The Oregon Death with Dignity Act

The Oregon Death with Dignity Act was a citizen's initiative first passed by Oregon voters in November 1994 with 51% in favor. Implementation was delayed by a legal injunction, but after proceedings that included a petition denied by the United States Supreme Court, the Ninth Circuit Court of Appeals lifted the injunction on October 27, 1997. In November 1997, a measure asking Oregon voters to repeal the Death with Dignity Act was placed on the general election ballot (Measure 51, authorized by Oregon House Bill 2954). Voters rejected this measure by a margin of 60% to 40%, retaining the Death with Dignity Act.

The Death with Dignity Act allows terminally-ill Oregon residents to obtain and use prescriptions from their physicians for self-administered, lethal medications. Under the Act, ending one's life in accordance with the law does not constitute suicide. However, we use the term "physician-assisted suicide" because it is used in the medical literature to describe ending life through the voluntary self-administration of lethal medications prescribed by a physician for that purpose. The Death with Dignity Act legalizes PAS, but specifically prohibits euthanasia, where a physician or other person directly administers a medication to end another's life.

To request a prescription for lethal medications, the Death with Dignity Act requires that a patient must be:

- An adult (18 years of age or older)
- A resident of Oregon
- Capable (defined as able to make and communicate health care decisions)
- Diagnosed with a terminal illness that will lead to death within 6 months

Patients meeting these requirements are eligible to request a prescription for lethal medication from a licensed Oregon physician. To receive a prescription for lethal medication, the following steps must be fulfilled:

- The patient must make two oral requests to their physician, separated by at least 15 days.
- The patient must provide a written, witnessed request to their physician (two witnesses).
- The prescribing physician and a consulting physician must confirm the diagnosis and prognosis.
- The prescribing physician and a consulting physician must determine whether the patient is capable.
- If either physician believes the patient's judgment is impaired by a psychiatric or psychological disorder, the patient must be

referred for a psychological examination.

- The prescribing physician must inform the patient of feasible alternatives to assisted suicide including comfort care, hospice care, and pain control.
- The prescribing physician must request, but may not require, the patient to notify their next-of-kin of the prescription request.

To comply with the law, physicians must report to the OHD all prescriptions for lethal medications. Reporting is not required if patients begin the request process but never receive a prescription. In the summer of 1999, the Oregon legislature added a requirement that pharmacists must be informed of the prescribed medication's ultimate use. Physicians and patients who adhere to the requirements of the Act are protected from criminal prosecution, and the choice of legal physician-assisted suicide cannot affect the status of a patient's health or life insurance policies. Physicians and health care systems are under no obligation to participate in the Death with Dignity Act.

The Reporting System

The OHD is required by the Act to develop a reporting system for monitoring and collecting information on PAS. To fulfill this mandate, the OHD uses a system involving physician prescription reports and death certificate reviews.

When a prescription for lethal medication is written, the physician must submit to the OHD information that documents compliance with the law. We review all physician reports and contact physicians regarding missing or discrepant data. OHD Vital Records files are searched periodically for death certificates that correspond to physician reports. These death certificates allow us to confirm patients' deaths, and provide patient demographic data (for example, age, place of residence, level of education).

For this report, we also included telephone interviews conducted with all prescribing physicians after receipt of their patients' death certificate. Each physician was asked to confirm whether the patient took the lethal medications. We also collected data that was not available from physician reports or death certificates—including insurance status and end-of-life care. We asked why the patient requested a prescription, specifically exploring concerns about the financial impact of the illness, loss of autonomy, decreasing ability to participate in activities that make life enjoyable, being a burden, loss of control of bodily functions, and uncontrollable pain. If the patient took the lethal medication, we collected information on the time to unconsciousness and death, and asked about any unexpected adverse reactions. Physicians are not legally required to be present when a patient ingests the medication, so not all have information about what happened when the patient ingested the medication.

Many terminally ill patients have more than one physician providing care at the end of life: to maintain consistency in data collection, we interviewed only prescribing physicians. Information about the prescribing physician—such as age, sex, number of years in practice, and medical specialty—was collected during the interviews. We do not interview or collect any information from patients prior to their death. Reporting forms and the physician questionnaire are available at www.ohd.hr.state.or.us/chs/pas/pas.htm.

We classified patients by year of participation based on when they ingested the legally-prescribed lethal medication. Using demographic information from 1999 Oregon death certificates, we compared patients who used legal PAS with other Oregonians who died from similar diseases. The proportion of deaths resulting from legal PAS was estimated for 2000 using total and disease-specific 1999 deaths in the denominator. . . .

Results

In 2000, 39 prescriptions for lethal doses of medication were written, compared with 24 in 1998 and 33 in 1999. Twenty-six of the third-year prescription recipients died after ingesting the medication; eight died from their underlying disease; five were alive on December 31, 2000. In addition, one 1999 prescription recipient died in 2000 after ingesting the medication (one 1999 prescription recipient was alive on December 31, 2000). The total number of patients who used PAS in 2000 was 27 (26 patients who received prescriptions in 2000, and 1 patient who received a prescription in 1999).

Based on death certificate data, patients participating in 2000 were similar to those in previous years, except that they were increasingly likely to be married. Of 13 third-year patients with at least a college degree, eight had post-baccalaureate education. In all three years most patients choosing PAS had cancer.

During 1999, a total of 29,356 Oregonians died. Thus, patients ingesting lethal medications in 2000 represented an estimated 9/10,000 total Oregon deaths. By comparison, 1998 PAS patients represented 6/10,000 deaths; 1999 PAS patients, 9/10,000 deaths. The 27 patients participating in 2000 resembled 6,981 other Oregonians who died from similar underlying illnesses with respect to age, race, and residence. However, as education increased so did likelihood of participation. Patients with a college education were eight times more likely to participate than people without a high school education; patients with post-baccalaureate education were 19 times more likely to participate than people without a high school education.

We interviewed the 22 physicians who legally prescribed lethal medications to the 27 PAS patients in 2000. Thirteen (59%) physicians were in family practice or internal medicine, five (23%) were oncologists, and four were in other specialties. Their median age was 50 years (range 34–58 years); their median years in practice, 21 (range

1–29 years). One physician was reported to the Oregon Board of Medical Examiners for submitting a written consent form with only one signature, although other witnesses were in attendance.

As in previous years, most of the patients who used PAS in 2000 were enrolled in hospice care. Of the three who declined hospice, two patients felt they did not need it, and one patient did not wish to stop treatment (a requirement for hospice). Almost all patients died at home. No patient died in an acute-care hospital. All patients in 2000 appeared to have some form of health insurance, though not all physicians knew the type of insurance. At least 16 (64%) of 25 patients with a known insurance type had private health insurance.

Physicians were present at 14 (52%) of the 27 legal PAS deaths. If they were not present, we accepted information they had based on discussions with family members, friends or other health professionals who attended the patients' deaths. Among the patients for whom we received information about the time of ingestion and death, half of the patients were unconscious within 9 minutes of taking the medication, and half died within 30 minutes. At least one patient was unconscious for up to six hours after ingesting the medication, but the actual time to death was not known. One patient regurgitated approximately 10 ml of secobarbitol suspension immediately after ingestion. This patient became unconscious within 1 minute of ingestion and died within 7 minutes. No physician reported activation of the emergency medical system after medication ingestion.

Physicians were asked if, based on discussions with patients, any of six end-of-life concerns might have contributed to the patients' requests for lethal medication. In all cases, physicians reported multiple concerns contributing to the request. Eleven (41%) patients included at least four specific concerns: becoming a burden, losing autonomy, decreasing ability to participate in activities that make life enjoyable, and losing control of bodily functions. Another 15 (56%) patients included at least two or three of these concerns. Most frequently noted across all three years were loss of autonomy (2000, 93%; 1999, 78%; 1998, 75%) and participation in activities that make life enjoyable (2000, 78%; 1999, 81%; 1998, 69%). Patients have increasingly expressed concern about becoming a burden to family friends or caregivers (2000, 63%; 1999, 26%; 1998, 12%). All but one patient expressing this concern in 2000 also expressed concern about losing autonomy. One patient concerned about the financial implications of treating or prolonging their illness was concerned about all other issues except pain control.

Comments

The numbers of patients choosing legal PAS has remained small over the last three years (6–9/10,000 Oregon deaths per year). While these numbers increased from the first year to the second, the third year's findings indicated that this increase was not part of a trend. In fact, the numbers of patients choosing PAS remained consistent from year two to year three. In each year, the proportion of PAS deaths as a subset of deaths due to terminal illnesses such as cancers is of the same magnitude as recently estimated by Emanuel, et al., and is consistent with numbers from a survey of Oregon physicians. Overall, smaller numbers of patients appear to use PAS in the U.S. compared to the Netherlands. However, as detailed in previous reports, our numbers are based on a reporting system for terminally ill patients who legally receive prescriptions for lethal medications, and do not include patients and physicians who may act outside the law.

After the first year's report, the relatively low proportion of married persons participating led to concerns that socially isolated patients might be more likely to use PAS than patients with better social support. An increasing proportion of married participants in years two and three now shows that the proportions of PAS patients married, widowed, divorced or never married resemble those seen among other Oregonians dying from similar diseases. Also, in the second year it was observed that college educated patients were 12 times more likely to choose PAS compared to patients with less than a high school degree. In this third year we considered patients with a post-baccalaureate education separately, and found the difference to be even greater. That educated patients are more likely to choose PAS is consistent with findings that Oregon patients with at least a college degree are more likely to be knowledgeable about end-of-life choices.

Concern about loss of autonomy and participation in activities that make life enjoyable have been consistently important motivating factors in patient requests for lethal medication. However, the proportion of patients expressing concern about becoming a burden has increased. Consistent with previous findings from family interviews, physicians in 2000 commented that family members were very willing to care for the patients. Interestingly, not being a burden was one of only eight end-of-life issues in a recent study rated as important by most patients but not most physicians. That Oregon PAS patients almost always discussed concern about becoming a burden in conjunction with losing autonomy suggests that it might be part of patients' ideas about independence. However, a negative interpretation of concern about becoming a burden is that patients may feel pressured by others into using PAS. No evidence indicates that such pressure has been a primary motivating influence among the 70 Oregon patients participating to date, but this possibility should be discussed by physicians, patients and family members.

PAS has become an important element in the national discussion on end-of-life care. In 2000, Oregon physicians who prescribed lethal medications commented frequently on the role of PAS in this respect. One physician was an opponent of PAS, but had decided that as a caregiver it was important to support the beliefs of the terminally ill patient. A second physician had previously turned down one patient, but the patient assisted in 2000 "called [the physician] out on his responsibility to provide PAS". Another physician wrote a prescription in consultation with a colleague who supported the patient's choice but felt uncomfortable providing the prescription itself. In each case, the patients were knowledgeable about end-of-life choices and had a complex set of end-of-life concerns contributing to their request. While the experiences of these few patients and physicians reflect a rarely chosen end-of-life care alternative, they provide an important source of insight to inform the national debate on end-of-life care.

TWO DEATHS IN OREGON

Christine J. Gardner

In this selection, Christine J. Gardner, a frequent writer for *Christianity Today* magazine, contrasts the lives and deaths of two Oregon men suffering from amyotrophic lateral sclerosis, an incurable disease that leaves people completely disabled at the end of life. One of the two took advantage of Oregon's Death with Dignity Act to obtain drugs with which to kill himself, Gardner explains, while the other, supported by his family and church, found no reason to hasten his death. Gardner believes that laws like Oregon's would be unnecessary if all terminally ill people were surrounded by loving family, friends, and church members.

Troy Thompson's future was coming into full focus. Marilyn, Thompson's tall, blond wife of 15 months, had just given birth to their daughter, Victoria. With three other daughters from their previous marriages, family life was satisfying and happy. Work brought fulfillment, too. As a landscape designer in Salem, Oregon, Thompson, 32, enjoyed bringing beauty to life. The Thompsons had recently purchased land on a hill overlooking the lush Willamette Valley in Newberg, a bedroom community of Portland. Their life's dream, including plans for a new house, seemed almost complete.

In 1993, a month after Victoria's birth, Thompson's life took an unexpected turn when he came home from work with a dull pain in his upper back. Strained muscles were nothing new for the six-foot-four outdoor enthusiast. But this time the muscle began to twitch in an unfamiliar way.

First, Thompson went to a physical therapist who, in May 1994, then sent him to a neurologist. He put Thompson through a battery of tests that included blood work and an MRI. Two weeks later, the neurologist had ruled out every possible cause except amyotrophic lateral sclerosis (ALS, also known as Lou Gehrig's disease). He referred the Thompsons to neurologist Wendy Johnston, Portland's top ALS specialist, at the Oregon Health Sciences University.

The Thompsons assumed Johnston would conduct more medical tests. They did not realize that the referral was, in fact, a diagnosis. Later that day, the Thompsons' family doctor called to express condolences upon hearing the news. The referring neurologist had been more candid with the family doctor than with the patient. Marilyn Thompson broke down in tears. "It was so sudden and so devastating. We weren't ready to believe it."

Dependent on God

The diagnosis was a death sentence. ALS, which destroys neurons that control muscle movement, would eventually leave Thompson's active mind trapped in a lifeless body.

About 30,000 Americans have ALS. Another 5,000 cases are diagnosed each year. The debilitating disease, which results in progressive paralysis, can move rapidly through the body in less than two years, but some patients live for more than ten years. There is no known cause of ALS and no known cure. It is always fatal.

Thompson's future—painful, immobile, and dependent—looked bleak. But a few months later, the State of Oregon gave him another option.

In November 1994, Oregon voters passed Ballot Measure 16, the "Death with Dignity Act," by a margin of 51 to 49 percent. For the first time in U.S. history, patients with six months left to live could ask their doctors for a prescription of lethal drugs to end their lives.

Within weeks of his first visit with Johnston, Thompson's speech began to slur and his hands began to curl. Determined to keep their lives moving forward, the Thompsons put their Lake Oswego home up for sale and began construction on their home in rural Newberg.

But by late 1994, Thompson, once an avid skier and fine-arts photographer, could no longer put on his coat by himself.

Daily life became a struggle. Long days and sleepless nights were filled with bed sores, feeding tubes, and oxygen tanks. Marilyn Thompson, who managed a team of real-estate agents, cut back to working three days a week; meanwhile, her husband worried about becoming a burden to his family. "It broke his heart," she recalls.

But Thompson, a committed Christian, did not consider physician-assisted suicide an option. As his independence slipped away, he became more dependent on God. His faith gave him the strength to resist the temptation of death's escape.

Help and Prayers

In January 1996, after the Thompsons moved into their new home, their doctor told Thompson he had less than six months to live. Hospice workers, extended family, church friends, and other caregivers began assisting Marilyn Thompson with her husband's care around the clock.

"It was really sacrificial," says Keith Reetz, assistant pastor of Beaverton Foursquare Church where the Thompsons attended. "It was unbelievable what people did for them in terms of service." A church member cleaned the Thompsons' house each week. Other members from various local churches prepared meals and bought groceries. Some gave money to help cover mounting medical bills.

Prayer teams visited regularly. Encircling Thompson's bed, they would lay hands on his motionless body and pray for healing. Prayer chains stretched from Canada to Spain.

Caregivers helped Thompson remain as independent as possible. With a special single-click mouse on his computer, he used his big toe to order flowers for his wife over the Internet. He communicated with the help of his computer's voice synthesizer, which "spoke" phrases he typed. Eventually, he could move only his eyebrows. Caregivers would painstakingly assemble words for him with the help of a spelling chart.

As Thompson clung to life, Christians in Oregon were losing the fight against physician-assisted suicide. After a legal injunction against the law was lifted in October 1997, Ballot Measure 51 was introduced in an attempt to repeal the law. In November 1997, the measure failed by a margin of 60 percent to 40 percent.

Thompson could now legally take his own life. A television news crew from Japan interviewed Thompson on the night of the vote. They wanted to know if he would request lethal drugs. Thompson typed in response, "God doesn't make mistakes. He is the author and finisher of our lives."

Eight months later, at age 36, on July 11, 1998, two days before he had been scheduled to testify as a plaintiff in a lawsuit against the State of Oregon to block the physician-assisted suicide law, Thompson died. Four people professed a new commitment to Christ at his memorial service.

"Thompson's a hero," says Reetz. "He's walking in the footsteps of Job. I can't picture Job opting for assisted suicide." Marion County, Thompson's employer, created the Troy Thompson Humanitarian Award to honor county employees who reflect his "commitment to life."

Nearly a year after his death, the Thompson family still mourns the loss of their husband and father. Five-year-old Victoria, whom her mother calls "Victory," or Tory for short, often talks of heaven. She pictures her daddy running and dancing, things she never saw him do in life. Marilyn Thompson cries softly when she talks about her "knight in shining armor." But she is grateful he lived longer than his doctors predicted. "People don't normally experience life at its most vital point," she says. "We would have missed some profound experiences.". . .

Lost Independence

In 1994, Pat Matheny was among the majority of Oregon voters who cast ballots for physician-assisted suicide. At the time, he did not realize the impact his vote would have on his life: three years later, at age 41, he was diagnosed with ALS.

Matheny, who worked as a cabinetmaker and assistant teacher at Head Start, lived in a travel trailer parked behind his parents' house in Coos Bay on the Oregon coast 200 miles south of Portland.

Strongly independent, Matheny served in the National Guard and earned his pilot's license, "just for the challenge of it," his parents recall. After more than a decade of woodworking, Matheny decided to enroll in college. He graduated with honors from the University of Oregon at age 39.

As with Thompson, Matheny visited ALS specialist Wendy Johnston, who gave him a prognosis similar to Thompson's. But Matheny had a sharply different reaction. "He had a combination of resignation and managed despair," Johnston recalls.

With Matheny's condition worsening, his mother, Patricia, acted as his primary caregiver, carrying an infant monitor around the house so she could respond to his needs. Each day, his mother would arrange ten cigarettes in a bowl, filter side pointing up. Matheny could pick them up with his mouth and light them with a foot-powered treadle pump. A small tabletop vise held Matheny's favorite foods—breakfast burritos, corn dogs, and Burger King Whoppers—allowing him to feed himself.

Within a year of his diagnosis, Matheny's condition had deteriorated rapidly. He lost the use of his arms. He had difficulty swallowing. Television became a constant companion. But he could still scoot around his trailer on the wheeled desk chair that he pushed with his feet. And he could e-mail friends and relatives with his foot-controlled computer. But he required assistance in bathing and dressing. Matheny felt the quality of his life slipping away.

Matheny feared losing autonomy more than he feared death. While not religious, he believed in reincarnation and the existence of a Supreme Being. Matheny considered overdosing on illegal drugs or shooting himself. Ultimately, Matheny decided to test the new law and kill himself lawfully.

He contacted the Hemlock Society for a doctor referral. Under the law's mandate, the process included two verbal requests from Matheny (separated by a 15-day waiting period), a written request, and the consent of two physicians. Matheny approached at least three physicians before finding one who would agree to give the second consent.

Making a Statement

In November 1998, Matheny received a package of barbiturates and antinausea pills in the mail. The prescription cost him $47. Matheny's insurance could have covered the cost of the medications. Instead, Matheny paid for them himself to protect his prescribing physician from controversy.

Matheny received some Christian literature in the mail from concerned individuals who wrote that they were praying for him. A hospice chaplain offered to meet with him, but Matheny rebuffed the chaplain's overtures.

At Christmas, the Matheny family, including Matheny's teenage son from an earlier marriage, gathered in Coos Bay to say a final goodbye. After an emotional holiday, Matheny decided the time had come. On December 28, Matheny asked his older brother, Michael, visiting from Florida, to take the drugs out of the refrigerator.

But choosing death turned out to be harder than Matheny imagined. Isolating himself in his trailer, Matheny agonized over his decision for a week. Then, on January 4, 1999, two days before his forty-third birthday, Matheny decided to wait.

Holding the power of death in his hands, Matheny determined his life still had meaning because his mind was still active. He wanted to help find a cure for ALS. He had developed a survey for ALS patients to help determine causes of the disease. He was also participating in a drug trial. In addition, he wanted to further the cause of physician-assisted suicide. Like the early Oregon pioneers, Matheny saw himself as a trailblazer into uncharted legal territory. But he knew his voice of support for physician-assisted suicide would be heard loudest only through his own death.

On March 8, Matheny's brother-in-law, Joe Hayes, arrived from Lincoln City, about 100 miles north of Coos Bay. Matheny's parents had asked Hayes to relieve them of Matheny's care for a few days. Two days later, Hayes told Patricia and Robert Matheny that their son had died. Matheny had asked for Hayes's help in taking the drugs because Matheny wanted to spare his parents the agony of watching their son die.

Hayes told them that he mixed the barbiturates into a chocolate protein drink at Matheny's request and held the straw to Matheny's lips. Hayes also shook Matheny to keep him awake so he could finish the lethal drink.

The Mathenys deeply miss their son, but they respect his decision. "He always said he would know when the time was right," Patricia Matheny recalls.

"He thought he was doing something for a cause he believed in," Robert Matheny says.

Patricia Matheny says the law provided hope to her son, knowing that he, not a debilitating disease, controlled his fate. "My son's death was with dignity, because it was his choice, his way, and at his time," she says. "I don't think we would've had our son as long as we did if that medication wouldn't have been available."

The Power of Love

The lives and deaths of Pat Matheny and Troy Thompson illustrate the burden of choices facing the seriously ill in Oregon. Both Matheny and Thompson suffered from ALS. Both men are now dead. Each chose how he would die, but only one chose when. In their separate journeys toward death, Matheny found his hope in the law; Thompson found his hope in the love of family, friends, and his faith in a God who heals.

Both relied on caregivers and computers for fleeting moments of independence. But only Thompson fully acknowledged his dependence on God, which allowed for an acceptance of his growing reliance on others. "He wasn't embarrassed or ashamed" of his illness, his wife says. Matheny mostly kept family and friends at bay, living alone in his trailer. "He always wanted to do things his way," his mother recalls.

Wendy Johnston counsels ALS patients to consider their growing needs as their gift to others. "In fiercely maintaining your independence, you are taking something away from your family," she says. "Accepting the help of others, letting your family care for you, can be something you give back to them."

The Thompson family prayed for Troy's physical healing, but the miracle appears to have occurred in and through the lives of those who knew him. "The Lord put so many people in their lives, just stationed them at critical points to provide the kind of support that they would need," pastor Keith Reetz recalls. "So they've got a zillion miracle stories. A lot of those are just through people."

The Thompsons received hundreds of grateful e-mail messages after the publicity of Troy's illness. One young father wrote that he had felt trapped in substance abuse and considered suicide. He said Thompson's story gave him the courage to live.

Marilyn Thompson credits Josh Henley, a caregiver in his midtwenties who worked with her husband for two and a half years, with helping to prolong his life through their friendship. Thompson became a spiritual mentor to Henley, who had fallen away from his Seventh-day Adventist upbringing. Henley was one of the four who made a commitment to Christ at Thompson's memorial service.

By contrast, Matheny had far fewer resources to sustain him, which troubles Johnston. She regrets that the distance between her office and Matheny's home prohibited her from offering more personalized care. She speculates that if Matheny would have had increased financial means, broader emotional support, and meaningful religious beliefs, he might have reached a different conclusion about the quality and meaning of his life.

The Church Reaches Out

So far, the church has been powerless to keep physician-assisted suicide off the Oregon law books. Pro-life groups such as Physicians for Compassionate Care and Americans for Integrated Palliative Care continue to challenge cost-conscious managed care in support of improved end-of-life care. . . .

In the interim, Christians are gaining small but vital victories in homes and in doctors' offices across the state. A Christian gynecologic oncologist [specialist in cancers that affect women] in Portland says business is up since he posted a statement in his waiting room that says he will not participate in assisted suicide.

As in the case of Thompson, the church is at its most powerful when its members minister one-on-one to the sick and dying. But many outreach efforts are focused on those already within the church body. Tangible expressions of Christ's love to the seriously ill could have their strongest impact on those outside the Christian community.

At least 16 individuals in Oregon, including Pat Matheny, have faced death and decided life was no longer worth living.

Churches in Oregon are rediscovering how to give people a reason to live. Reetz, the Thompsons' pastor, is convinced that the mission fields of the future are hospitals, convalescent centers, and the homes of the sick and dying.

Acts of compassion, not quick deathbed conversions, are the motivation. "All we can do is make ourselves available and reach out," he says.

Yet Reetz readily acknowledges that not everyone will accept the hope the church offers. "That's the heartbreaking side of it."

Psychiatric Evaluation of Euthanasia Requests in an Oncology Clinic

Marjolein Bannink, Arthur R. Van Gool, Agnes van der Heide, and Paul J. van der Maas

Bannink and coauthors, all physicians in Rotterdam, the Nether-lands, report on psychiatric evaluations of twenty-two cancer patients who requested euthanasia between June 1997 and June 1999. They conclude that such evaluation, based on the Royal Dutch Medical Association's guidelines, can help in determining which people have a "longstanding and well-considered wish to die" and therefore should be granted their wish. However, they say, it is not valuable enough to be required in all cases. Bannink and Van Gool work at the University Hospital Rotterdam-Daniel, and van der Heide and van der Maas are in the Department of Public Health of Erasmus University.

The role of undiagnosed psychiatric disorders in patients requesting euthanasia is an important ethical and professional issue. From June, 1997, until June, 1999, we included a psychiatric consultation as part of our standard procedure for handling euthanasia requests. Of 22 cancer patients who requested euthanasia at short notice: ten had their longstanding and well-considered wish for euthanasia granted; six were denied euthanasia because they did not have such a wish; five were denied because of psychiatric problems; and one was granted the wish despite minor psychiatric symptoms. Our findings suggest that a psychiatrist should be consulted if the treatment team has doubts about a patient's state of mind.

The standard practice for handling euthanasia requests at the University Hospital Rotterdam-Daniel is based on the Royal Dutch Medical Association's procedural guidelines, and establishes whether or not demands originate from a longstanding and well-considered wish to die. From June 1, 1997, until June 1, 1999, psychiatric consultation was added to this standard procedure, to determine whether appeals for euthanasia were influenced by psychiatric problems. During these

2 years, we (MB, AVG) were consulted by twelve female and ten male cancer patients who requested euthanasia at short notice. The mean age of these patients was 60 years (range 37–77).

Following consultation, ten individuals were thought to have a longlasting and well-considered wish for euthanasia that did not originate from undue pressure from others or intolerable pain. Additionally, none of the patients had current psychiatric disorders, although three had a history of psychiatric problems. The patients' requests were therefore granted, though three died from natural causes before the date set for euthanasia. The remainder died as a result of euthanasia either at home (four) or in hospital (three).

In six of the 22 patients, all women with no psychiatric disorders, consultation with a psychiatrist established that the request for euthanasia had not been fully considered. One patient's appeal seemed to be based on inaccurate medical information received before she was transferred to our hospital and, after adequate diagnostic testing and discussion of results, she withdrew her request. Four other patients did not sustain their requests for euthanasia after examination by the psychiatrist; they seemed to regard euthanasia, or having the option of euthanasia, as a way to control their feelings of despair, pain, and helplessness. According to the psychiatrist and the primary physician, their appeals were mainly aimed at explicitly discussing their situation with the attending physician, to reduce anxiety and insecurity. The sixth patient agreed to wait 4 days to be able to further discuss her request for euthanasia with the primary oncologist most acquainted with her case, who was abroad. She died before he returned.

The final six patients, all men, showed psychiatric symptoms. Of these, five had cognitive or depressive disorders, which decreased their competence in decision thinking. Since these diagnoses concurred with doubts about the durability of the request, euthanasia was denied. Four of these patients died from natural causes within a week of psychiatric consultation, and one died from natural causes in a nursing home 4 months later.

In two of these cases the primary physician had underestimated the influence of a psychiatric disorder on patient competence and decision-making abilities, and had considered complying with the request. In both cases the psychiatrist's involvement changed the policy and euthanasia was denied. One patient had depressive symptoms and slight cognitive impairment, but not to a degree which implicated impaired decision-making capacities. Because his request was in line with earlier expressed explicit opinions on his illness and his impending death, and his wish for autonomy, we agreed to comply with his wishes. This patient died as a result of euthanasia.

Of 22 patients who requested euthanasia therefore, eight died according to their wishes and two were denied euthanasia as a direct result of psychiatric consultation. By not complying with the wish of these terminally ill patients we neither lengthened not shortened their lives, but did alter the way in which they died. In our opinion, this result does not automatically imply that standard psychiatric consultation should be mandatory. The benefits of such consultation should be balanced against the disadvantages of pushing the psychiatrist to the fore as the final gatekeeper. However, in general, staff appreciate the expertise, help, and support given by a consultant psychiatrist, who might add to the quality of the decision-making process in specific cases.

Assisted Suicide and Euthanasia in the Netherlands

Herbert Hendin

In testimony given before a Congressional subcommittee on April 29, 1996, Herbert Hendin describes the dangers he sees in the fact that euthanasia and assistance in suicide are relatively easy to obtain in the Netherlands. He points out, for example, that physicians sometimes carry out euthanasia even when patients have not requested it. Hendin, who opposes assisted suicide and euthanasia, is a professor of psychiatry at New York Medical College and medical director of the American Foundation for Suicide Prevention. His most recent book is *Seduced by Death: Doctors, Patients, and Assisted Suicide.*

Most people assume that seriously or terminally ill people who wish to end their lives are different than those who are otherwise suicidal. But the first reaction of many patients to the diagnosis of serious illness and possible death is terror, depression, and a wish to die. Such patients are not significantly different than patients who react to other crises in their lives with the desire to end the crisis by ending their lives.

Suicidal patients are also prone to make conditions on life: I won't live . . . "without my husband," . . ."if I lose my looks, power, prestige or health," or "if I am going to die soon." They are afflicted by the need to make demands on life that cannot be fulfilled.

Determining the time, place, and circumstances of their death is the most dramatic expression of their need for control. The request for assisted suicide is also usually made with as much ambivalence as are most suicide attempts. If the doctor does not recognize the ambivalence as well as the anxiety and depression that underlie patients' requests for death, the patient may become trapped by that request and die in a state of unrecognized terror.

Empowering Doctors, Not Patients

I have just completed a study of assisted suicide and euthanasia in the Netherlands where both are accepted practices. In the past decade by

Reprinted from Herbert Hendin's testimony before the U.S. House Committee on the Judiciary, Subcommittee on the Constitution, April 29, 1996.

making assisted suicide and euthanasia easily available to those over 50 the Dutch have reduced the suicide rate in this segment of their population.

Among an older population physical illness of all types is common, and many who have trouble coping with physical illness became suicidal. In a culture accepting of euthanasia their distress is accepted as a good reason for dying. It may be more than ironic to describe euthanasia as the Dutch cure for suicide.

Should we consider legalization of assisted suicide an extension of the patients' rights movement? That it is often the doctor and not the patient who determines the choice for death was underlined by the documentation of "involuntary euthanasia" in the Remmelink report—the Dutch government's commissioned study of the problem.

The report [published in 1991] revealed that in over 1,000 cases, of the 130,000 deaths in the Netherlands each year, physicians admitted they actively caused or hastened death without any request from the patient. In about 5,000 cases physicians made decisions that might or were intended to end the lives of competent patients without consulting them.

I was given an example of a case where this was necessary—a doctor who had terminated the life of a nun who was dying in great pain but whose religious convictions did not permit her to ask for death. Even when the patient requests or consents to euthanasia, in cases presented to me in the Netherlands and cases I have reviewed in this country, assisted suicide and euthanasia were usually the result of an interaction in which the needs and character of family, friends, and doctor play as big and often bigger role than those of the patient.

A study of euthanasia done in Dutch hospitals concluded that in most cases families, doctors, and nurses were involved in pressuring patients to request euthanasia.

A Dutch medical journal described a wife who no longer wished to care for her sick husband; she gave him a choice between euthanasia and admission to a home for the chronically ill. The man, afraid of being left to the mercy of strangers in an unfamiliar place, chose to be killed. The doctor, although aware of the coercion, ended the man's life.

The Remmelink report revealed that more than half of Dutch physicians considered it appropriate to introduce the subject of euthanasia to their patients. They seemed not to recognize that the doctor was also telling the patient that his or her life was not worth living, a message that would have a powerful effect on the patient's outlook and decision.

Patients who request euthanasia are usually asking in the strongest way they know for mental and physical relief from suffering. When that request is made to a caring, sensitive, and knowledgeable physician who can address their fear, relieve their suffering, and assure them that he or she will remain with them to the end, most patients no longer want to die and are grateful for the time remaining to them.

But in the Netherlands social sanction has encouraged patients and doctors to see assisted suicide and euthanasia—intended as an unfortunate necessity in exceptional cases—as almost a routine way of dealing with serious or terminal illness. The public has the illusion that legalizing assisted suicide and euthanasia will give them greater autonomy. If the Dutch experience teaches us anything it is that euthanasia enhances the power and control of doctors who can suggest it, not give patients obvious alternatives, ignore patients' ambivalence, and even put to death patients who have not requested it.

CHAPTER 5

RELIGION, ETHICS, AND EUTHANASIA

RELIGION SOMETIMES PERMITS HASTENED DEATH

Courtney S. Campbell

Courtney S. Campbell claims that although most major religions forbid suicide, many accept people's right not to prolong life in all circumstances. Some groups, he maintains, even feel that hastening death through assisted suicide or euthanasia is acceptable under some conditions. Campbell is a professor of philosophy at Oregon State University and director of the university's Program for Ethics, Science, and the Environment. He has coedited several books on bioethics and is a former editor of the *Hastings Center Report*, a journal devoted to ethics.

The advance of technologies to prolong life and control dying can raise agonizing moral dilemmas. What guidance is offered by the great world religions?

In "The Parable of the Mustard Seed", the Buddha teaches a lesson that is valid for all cultures: human beings receive no exemption from mortality. Deep in the throes of grief after the death of her son, a woman seeks wisdom from the Buddha, who says that he does indeed have an answer to her queries. Before giving it, however, he insists that she must first collect a grain of mustard seed from every house that has not been touched by death. She canvasses her entire community, but fails to collect a single seed. Returning to the Buddha, she understands that, like all other living beings, we are destined to die.

Death is a defining characteristic of human experience. Yet, while the event of death remains elusively beyond human control, the process of dying has increasingly been brought into the domain of medicine and life-extending technologies. Some technologies, including organ transplantation, respirators, antibiotics like penicillin, and feeding tubes, enable life to be prolonged. Other technologies may hasten death.

The decision to use these technologies is a moral choice, because it involves a decision about a fundamental human good, the preservation of life. Yet, in some situations, a resort to technology to stave off death comes at a price of compromising another fundamental

From "Euthanasia and Religion," by Courtney S. Campbell, *UNESCO Courier*, January 2000. Reprinted with permission.

human value, the quality of that life. Decisions about continuing treatment for the dying or of allowing death to take place by foregoing or terminating such treatment, or even by physician-assisted suicide or euthanasia are thus both existentially and ethically agonizing. As individuals and their families face these controversial questions and as many countries consider revising their laws on end-of-life choices, religious traditions and values can offer guidance and insight, if not solutions.

Historically, religious communities have sought to appropriate death within the life cycle through rituals of remembrance, and religious teachings have emphasized that death brings meaning to mortality. The process of dying is often portrayed as an invitation to spiritual insight and a key moment in the cultivation of spiritual identity.

The world's great traditions of moral wisdom all begin with a strong predisposition to favour the preservation of life, although the specific reasons for this conviction vary from tradition to tradition. Turning first to three monotheistic religious traditions which have had global influence, Judaism, Christianity and Islam, for all their differences, basically address ethical issues concerning the end of life from a common value perspective. In particular, discussions centre on the values of sovereignty, stewardship, and the self.

Sovereignty denotes that the lives and bodies of persons are created by, and ultimately return to, God. We owe our existence to a loving Being who has graciously brought us into being. Thus, the fundamental passages in human life, including birth and death, are of divine concern. This understanding of sovereignty has significant implications for decision-making at the end of life. It bestows sacredness upon human life, which supports the impulse towards preserving life by available medical technologies. Yet sovereignty also entails that the ultimate authority for deciding our mortal passages belongs to God. Human beings must not overstep these boundaries, or so to speak "play God" with life and death.

"Agents of God"

Through the value of stewardship, we are considered "agents of God", called to carry out the work of divine intent on earth. This task entails decision-making responsibilities for which we are accountable: our actions either further or violate divine intent. In addition, as emphasized in Islamic teaching, we are the trustees or stewards of our bodies. We are therefore entrusted with the capacities and responsibility to make appropriate decisions when confronting a treatment choice at the end of our own life or that of a loved one.

Indeed, with very few exceptions, the major faith traditions of the West have rejected a view known as "vitalism", which holds that biological life is to be preserved at all costs and with all available technologies. Vitalism is considered theologically mistaken because it appears to make divine will and intent contingent upon the state of medical technology. In other words, it puts technology in the role of God.

The dignity of persons, linked to the notion of "self", is another core value of these monotheistic faith traditions. In Jewish and Christian thought, this is expressed in the idea that humans are distinctively in the "image of God". Islamic theology does not use such language, but no less affirms the significant value of persons. The "religious self" is constituted in part by the person's rationality, freedom, and decision-making capacity, but also by relationships (with loved ones, for example) and bodily integrity. These characteristics support human responsibility in addressing end of life decisions, including refusals of medical procedures that invade the body with no real benefit, in the context of a caring community. Put another way, preserving life is not an absolute good in and of itself. Life is a good that opens the way to achieving higher goods that constitute the religious self.

So by looking within the moral parameters set by these three values of sovereignty, stewardship, and the self, we find that a patient can decide to forego life support. A doctor can also allow a patient to die if the continuation of life (by technological means) assaults the dignity of the person—if it attacks their rationality, freedom, relationships with others or their bodily integrity. Certainly, differences can be discerned between these traditions precisely over the priority of these goods. For example, Orthodox Jewish thought emphasizes the sanctity of life (as displayed in bodily integrity) which translates into a stronger commitment to life-extending technologies than in Roman Catholicism, which stresses the capacity for human relationships as a threshold for determining the permissibility of stopping life support.

Conflicts About Aid in Dying

The monotheistic faiths have also focused a great deal on the legalization of physician assistance in hastening death by providing a terminally ill patient with a lethal prescription of medication. In each instance, arguments supporting physician-assisted suicide have to overcome a longstanding prohibition of suicide. For a variety of reasons, suicide is sinful according to the three traditions. Suicide constitutes a wrong against one's nature and personal dignity ("religious self"). It also harms the community and violates the sovereignty of God. As a result, a physician assisting in suicide may be seen as a moral accomplice in evil, undermining the sacred covenant of the healer.

However, some faith communities in Protestant Christianity and in Reformed Judaism have argued otherwise. When faced with terminal illness, one may well be disposed to ending life, and one's immediate community (or family) may support this method of death. These kinds of arguments stress the dignity of the individual as a free decision-maker (which also applies to persons entrusted with the decision-making responsibilities of others). This dignity provides the basis for a political and philosophical claim to self-determination and opens the possibility for choosing the timing, circumstances and method of one's death. So physicians may be permitted to hasten death by pre-scribed medications, or even by administering lethal medication. Yet they would never be obligated to do so.

Many religious communities have denounced the question of legalizing physician euthanasia, or administrating death. The most vigorous opposition has come from the Roman Catholic tradition, with Pope John Paul II describing euthanasia as an example of the "culture of death" in Western societies. The Pope believes euthanasia is a manifestation of social views that have abandoned the protection of life and lent support to liberalized abortion, capital punishment, and incessant warfare.

In general, much religious opposition is based on concern for patients who may be in vulnerable positions because of their illness or their lack of social and economic resources. There is fear that patients who cannot afford expensive treatment, for example, will be pres-sured to accept euthanasia. There is also great concern about the moral nature of the doctor's professional self. Islamic teaching, for example, stresses the physician's commitment or covenant to healing. Euthanasia would violate this sacred role.

Although few in number, there are individual theologians within both the Jewish and Christian traditions for whom euthanasia is not a contradiction but a culmination of religious values such as com-passion, mercy, and love. By joining these values to respect for self-determination, some theologians can find a way of tolerating euthanasia as a final resort.

Eastern Faith Traditions

To die well, say the teachers of Eastern religions, one must live well. The views of Eastern religious traditions and philosophies have been very influential in global understanding about providing appropriate care to the dying. For example, the pioneering work of the Swiss-born psychiatrist Dr. Elisabeth Kubler-Ross in understanding the experiences of dying patients in Western medical institutions drew directly on understandings of the meaning of "good death" and "stages" in life in Hindu tradition. Buddhist values of compassion, non-violence, and suffering have also influenced the discourse of Western medical ethics. The ethical tension in these two traditions about end-of-life choices is rooted in two main values, liberation and ahimsa (non-violence).

In Hinduism and Buddhism, human beings are captured in end-less cycles of rebirth and reincarnation (karma-samsara). The goal of mortal life is detachment from the material world, culminating in the liberation of the true self from the body-mind complex. To expe-rience the good life and the good death, we must be constantly aware of the ultimate trajectory towards liberation.

In both traditions, all living creatures (humans, animals, plants, etc.) represent manifestations of the laws of karmic rebirth. To honour these laws, one must show great respect for the preservation of life and non-injury of sentient beings. Acts destructive of life are morally condemned by the principle of ahimsa, which is the conceptual equivalent of the Western principle of the sanctity of life. In most circumstances ahimsa bears a moral bias towards life-preservation. Yet there is some ethical flexibility which opens the possibility of foregoing treatment or seeking assistance to hasten death.

As a general rule, both Hinduism and Buddhism oppose suicide as an act of destroying life. However, a distinction is made in both traditions between self-regarding (or self-destructive) reasons and other-regarding (or compassionate) motives for seeking death. To commit suicide over the loss of a child or because of economic hardship (self-regarding reasons) is to commit a morally reprehensible act which reflects the individual's ignorance about the nature of life and human destiny. Instead of achieving the ultimate spiritual goal of liberation, a person who acts in this way will remain trapped in the ongoing karmic cycle of life-death-rebirth. Those who assist in this suicide may also be subject to karmic punishment, for they have violated the principle of ahimsa.

Compassion and Liberation

However, a very different perspective emerges when individuals seek death for spiritual motives, of which there are basically two kinds. The first revolves around compassion; concern for the welfare of others as one is dying can be seen as a sign of spiritual enlightenment. So a person can decide to forego treatment to avoid imposing a heavy burden of caregiving on family or friends. He or she may also stop treatment to relieve loved ones of the emotional or economic distress of prolonged dying.

The spiritual goal of liberation can also be seen as an ethical reason for seeking or hastening death. When physical suffering impedes self-control and lucidity, it is permissible to shorten life. Pain or lethargy might cloud the awareness and consciousness at death that both Hindus and Buddhists believe is necessary to ensure a favourable rebirth. Extreme suffering might also cause someone to be so attached to their material life (bodily condition) that they cannot pursue the ultimate spiritual goal of liberation from the material world.

This pattern of reasoning—the primacy of spiritual goals of liberation or compassion relative to the preservation of life—also applies to euthanasia through physician injection or administration of a lethal drug. Hindu and Buddhist scholars have found support for this so-called "active" euthanasia in their traditions by reflecting on the meaning of death as a door to liberation, the culmination of life in detachment from the material world. They then go a step further by linking compassion to the norm of self-similitude: "one should act towards others as one would have them act toward oneself". So euthanasia can be seen as a compassionate act or a "mercy killing" for a dying person striving to the highest purpose of human destiny, liberation.

A moral problem arises with euthanasia, however, if the administered medication renders the patient unconscious or unable to comprehend their descent toward death. The patient is unaware precisely at the moment when he or she should be most sensitive and receptive to spiritual teaching and meaning. For these reasons, other modes of bringing about death are preferable morally and religiously.

WHY CHRISTIANS REJECT ASSISTED SUICIDE

Gary L. Thomas

Gary L. Thomas offers the views of a moral theologian, a medical ethicist, a lawyer, and a physician specializing in the treatment of the aged to explain why Christians feel that physician-assisted suicide is unethical. These four experts belong to different Christian sects. Thomas quotes their suggested alternatives to assisted suicide. Thomas has written *Seeking the Face of God*, which draws on classic Christian writings to formulate a spirituality that can deal with everyday modern life.

Some support physician-assisted suicide out of fear of a lonely, pain-filled death. Here are four professionals who are making the dying a part of the church's ministry.

A Michigan physician thought carefully about what he would say to a cancer patient about the results of his latest tests. The news was not so good—his patient was near death and needed to be told so directly. This part of the job never became easy—it was never "routine." As gently as possible, the doctor started to speak. But the patient cut in: "Please don't tell me you'll be willing to talk about physician-assisted suicide," the patient pled. "I just don't want to hear it."

The doctor was shocked. Assisted suicide was the last thing on his mind, but in Michigan, the chosen haunt of assisted-suicide specialist Jack Kevorkian, it is apparently on many dying patients' minds—and it is radically changing their feelings about their physicians.

Diane Komp, a hematologist/oncologist [physician who specializes in blood diseases and cancer] at Yale University and a popular Christian author, has for years gone by the moniker "Doctor Di." In the course of a book and speaking tour through Michigan in the fall of 1996, several emcees made nervous references to "Doctor Die." As it happened again and again, Komp realized that physician-assisted suicide (PAS) advocates had accomplished just what they set out to do: For good or for ill, physician-assisted suicide was now on everybody's mind.

Advocates of physician-assisted suicide have tapped into the frightened psyche of our aging and ailing population, addressing a fear that, unfortunately, politicians, physicians, and the church are refusing to address: We die differently than we used to, and many of the elderly have plenty to fear.

Less than a century ago, death was spread fairly evenly across most age groups. Because we could not control bacteria very well and accidents were more common, a 10-year-old was scarcely more likely to survive to age 20 than a 40-year-old was to reach age 50. Today, all that has changed. Those of us who survive infancy and the accident-prone late teens and early twenties are likely to live well into our eighties; when we die, we will likely do so after a protracted illness that exhausts our life savings.

Massive social pressure and enterprising individuals are converging to force us to address this new reality of dying, and our society is actively revisiting a question that once needed little or no debate: Why should we oppose physician-assisted suicide?

Four professionals give us their perspective from the frontlines of this new reality. These individuals come from different traditions (evangelical, Roman Catholic, and mainline Protestant) and different vocations (a moral theologian, a medical ethicist, a lawyer, and a geriatrician [physician who specializes in treating old people]). Each one has a different perspective on the sobering end-of-life challenges facing our society.

A Different Way of Death

Allen Verhey, professor of religion at Hope College in Holland, Michigan, was confronted by a question that many of us will face. His parents—both of whom are still alive—asked him to exercise on their behalf a durable power of attorney for health care. Verhey's specialty is medical ethics, and he is well acquainted with the issues that such a responsibility raises—when to refuse treatment, the management of pain, and the growing controversies surrounding how we die.

"We die more slowly today," Verhey notes. "Even worse, we do it in hospitals, surrounded by technology rather than by friends and family. And this is what makes it especially frightening to some people."

When Verhey first began teaching medical ethics in the early seventies, PAS was not discussed that much. There was a "clear consensus" about the immorality of PAS. What he did speak (and write) about was a growing "shallowness of effort" in medical ethics, which looked to "generic principles." Verhey's book *Amoral Medicine* argued that medicine was losing its moral foundations and required religious traditions to guide it.

Verhey served for a time as the director of the Institute of Religion at the Texas Medical Center, providing him with the opportunity to pursue his "passion in the academy," which is to "retrieve religious traditions" as relevant to medical ethics. The fact that Verhey began teaching in Kevorkian's state in the late 1990s has pushed the particular problem of PAS to the forefront. But the thought behind Kevorkian's actions has been building for decades as people have encountered stories of how other people have died.

"There is a kind of 'I don't want to die the way Aunt Sarah did,'" Verhey points out, "and in order to gain some control over that happening, people are beginning to insist more and more on their own right to determine the conditions of their dying."

Moreover, "freedom has become the most important value in our society," and PAS is being touted as a way to provide people with yet more freedom. "Then the argument becomes, 'Who can be against maximizing freedom in this culture?'"

An Essential Distinction

The foundational issue, however—one that seems to determine a person's position on PAS—is that "the distinction between killing and allowing someone to die is less compelling than it once was." It was one thing in the late seventies and early eighties to discuss refusing or discontinuing heroic medical treatment, which is now uncontroversial; but today such refusal is being likened to the intentional killing of sick people. This moral leap is at the root of the pressure to legalize PAS and it is in part what drives Verhey to address it today. The Christian story, he points out, has traditionally preserved a sort of "dialectic about life" in which life is viewed as "a great gift," but not as the greatest good.

"This dialectic is woven through Scripture's narrative from Adam's first breath in the garden to sanctions against killing after the Flood, to the prohibition against murder in the Ten Commandments and, not least, to the significance of an empty tomb. It's clear that God intends life and that God's cause is life, not death. At the same time, because the Cross stands at the center of the story, Christians may not regard their own survival as the law of their being." The Christian tradition has sought to express this dialectic by prohibiting suicide while accepting death.

But this distinction is being assaulted by a culture that has a myopic [nearsighted] concern about consequences. "When we focus on consequences alone," Verhey warns, "the distinction [between active and passive euthanasia] isn't very compelling. Whether someone is killed or allowed to die, the consequence is the same [death]; so the distinction appears trivial, like moral nitpicking."

But to Verhey it is anything but moral nitpicking. He has been involved in questions about the refusal of treatment for some time, raising his "pastoral sensibilities" on the issue, and these sensibilities have led Verhey to become concerned that the new technologies surrounding a dying patient have not only increased physicians' and patients' options, but they have also taken one option away: the option of staying alive without having to justify one's existence. In other words, Verhey warns, the society that approves PAS under the guise of freedom may usher in a future in which suffering patients are no longer asked why they want to die, but why they want to go on living.

Though he served on a panel in April with PAS-advocate Dr. Timothy Quill, Verhey is adamant that it is not enough simply to engage in arguments. The Christian response to PAS must not be simply "to shout the prohibition." Churches should bear witness to their convictions and the biblical narrative that forms them by the way it cares for the dying. "The Christian community has the responsibility to model a better way to deal with dying than either keeping the patient alive as long as possible or eliminating a patient's suffering by eliminating the sufferer."

Meeting the Needs of the Dying

Working with the dying is a regular part of Edmund Pellegrino's medical practice. He has, at times, been asked to "assist" a patient in dying. Pellegrino's response to one such request is typical: After the patient expressed his wish, Pellegrino sought to meet the real needs behind the request.

First, he used the best methods of pain relief and increased the patient's sense of control by enabling the patient to self-administer the pain medication. This patient was also feeling guilty, clinically depressed, and concerned about being a burden to others. Pellegrino treated the depression, brought in a pastoral counselor to address the guilt, and gathered the patient's family to help them see how their response to this man's illness was aggravating his sense of unworthiness.

Once these needs were met, the patient thanked Pellegrino for not responding to his earlier request to die. "The most valuable days of my life have been the last days I have spent," he said.

Pellegrino approaches PAS on the wave of a long and storied career, having taught for over 50 years. He is currently professor of medicine and medical ethics at the Georgetown University Medical Center and is consulted regularly on issues surrounding medical ethics, particularly as they relate to the dying.

In Pellegrino's experience, the demand for PAS is a shortcut that attempts to address legitimate concerns in illegitimate ways. That is why he believes it is important to maintain the distinction between active and passive euthanasia, or, as he prefers to call it, between killing and letting die. However, as a professor who regularly engages in debate with leading PAS advocates, Pellegrino acutely understands that such a distinction is increasingly less respected by medical and public attitudes.

Pellegrino believes that underlying this erosion is a general assault on traditional medical ethics that was unleashed in the turbulent sixties. "The benign authoritarianism of traditional medical ethics gave way to participatory democracy. All of the sudden, people wanted to be involved in decisions that affected them." This converged with the civil-rights movement, the consumer movement, and the fight for women's and others' rights, shifting the focus of decision making from the physician to the patient and her family.

Now the situation is worsening as the economic pressure of "managed care" programs has entered the picture. Hardly a week goes by when Pellegrino isn't approached by another physician who is struggling with the ethical issues raised by managed care. Doctors feel caught between their loyalty to the patient and to the managed care corporation.

In such a climate, Pellegrino is particularly concerned that adding PAS to a doctor's options would be disastrous for many at-risk patients. "In this era of managed care, economic pressures may put the seriously ill infant, the elderly and senile, or the retarded at serious risk from distorted compassion." Pleas for assistance in suicide are in reality "desperate pleas for help, including emotional and spiritual support." They should therefore be met with "comprehensive, intensive, palliative care, not the accelerated demise of the person suffering."

Moral Abandonment

Pellegrino takes issue with those who see PAS as an act of compassion. "It is often more compassionate for the frustrated physician or hurting family than it is for the patient. In fact, assisted suicide is really a noncompassionate form of moral abandonment."

The specter of PAS goes beyond individual cases, however, to encompass a radical reworking of medical ethics. In Pellegrino's mind, it is the same radical reworking that has resulted in legalized abortion and in states such as Illinois and California insisting that physicians participate in state-ordered executions.

"What I'm talking about is the integrity of medical ethics, which must be independent of what either the state or law says it is. We need to examine the presuppositions, be aware of the conclusions they lead to, and detect in our own society any sign of the eroding of the substantial integrity of the ethics of medicine which has persisted for twenty-five hundred years: thou shalt not kill the patient, thou shalt not perform an abortion, and thou shalt act in the best interests of the patient."

Though he still hopes people are responsive to moral argument ("Otherwise, I wouldn't be teaching and writing about it"), Pellegrino expects that euthanasia will eventually be legalized. "We have already disassembled most of traditional medical ethics," he concedes.

In Pellegrino's mind, history, medical ethics, and contemporary experiments in countries such as the Netherlands all point to the fact that once a form of PAS is legalized, we will begin a desensitizing process that will inexorably lead us from bad to worse. "The Dutch are not malevolent people by nature, yet they're sliding down the slippery slope."

Pellegrino has followed the legalization of PAS in the Netherlands because he sees it as a "living laboratory of what happens when a society accepts the legitimacy of PAS. You've got direct, empirical evidence." And there Pellegrino has found that "the reports of the Dutch government and the Dutch Medical Society provide ample evidence that the slippery slope is no myth but a reality."

In its Remmelink report [published in 1991], the Dutch government documented that 1,000 persons were killed without giving consent in what was supposed to be a "voluntary" program. And "there is nothing in the second Dutch report [released in 1995] to suggest that this is not still occurring." In fact, the second report explained that the eligibility for PAS had been extended from terminally ill patients to include children, severely depressed patients, and elderly persons who weren't satisfied with the quality of their lives.

"The Netherlands experience shows that euthanasia cannot be contained by regulation and that most advocates reason that it would be 'merciful' to extend it here and there in individual cases," Pellegrino explains. "Any time we deem any human life as of unacceptable quality—the infant with cerebral damage, the retarded, the chronically and terminally ill—we make that life a target for 'merciful destruction' and accelerate the slide down the slippery slope to involuntary euthanasia."

A particularly chilling example of such "desensitization" exhibited itself when Pellegrino talked with a physician from the Netherlands. "How does it feel to do euthanasia?" he asked the euthanasiast.

"It's hard the first time," the doctor responded.

Protecting the Disabled

When Robert Destro went to work for the Catholic League for Religious and Civil Rights, he began focusing almost full-time on cases involving treatment given to the disabled. One in particular jolted his conscience. A young California boy with Down syndrome [a form of developmental disability] needed a heart operation, but the boy's father wanted to withhold treatment. Why fix the heart valve? the father asked. The boy was retarded.

Destro was outraged. "Are we going to stand by and watch this child die of medical neglect simply because he's retarded?" he asked.

Unbelievably, the state of California sided with the boy's father. Destro was shaken by the "amazing ignorance with respect to the reality of people who live with disabilities.

"From that moment on, I could see the progression of cases coming," Destro remembers.

The issue for Destro has always been "On what grounds will we deny basic rights to people with disabilities?"

In the Baby Doe case [a 1982 case concerning treatment of a severely disabled infant], the answer was couched in euphemisms such as "parental rights." But it was obvious to Destro that such arguments "always seem to favor the people who are young, beautiful, and flawless. Euphemisms provide cover for behavior which is not yet socially acceptable. It would not be socially or politically correct to argue that parents have a right to starve or deny necessary treatment to a child simply because he or she is retarded or has a physical disability, so they avoid the issue. 'Parental rights' is as good a cover as any."

What concerns Destro is the acceptance of a "hierarchy of disabilities," with mental disabilities at the bottom, and blindness and deafness at the top. The latter are seen as severe inconveniences, but the former are too often perceived as rendering the person who has them less "dignified" simply because they are dependent upon others for their care. The Australian bioethicist Peter Singer went so far as to question the humanity of the mentally disabled, arguing that since dogs and pigs are more intelligent than newborn babies, infanticide should be permitted whenever it is clear that the baby will never function as a "full" ("Whatever that means," Destro adds) human being.

If we allow inhumane treatment to begin anywhere in this hierarchy, Destro fears, we will become unable to draw any line at all. "Disabilities are tangible things—they inhibit a person's ability to do certain things—but a disability doesn't make them any less a person or any less a member of the community who is entitled to the same protection under the law as you or I."

It's ironic, Destro notes, that at the same time our federal government was passing the Americans with Disabilities Act [in 1990] and state legislatures all over the country were recognizing that persons with disabilities are full members of the community, the courts began taking the position that certain persons with disabilities are not worth keeping alive. The trend began in earnest when people in persistent vegetative states—such as Karen Ann Quinlan and Nancy Cruzan—were starved by withholding food and water on the grounds that they would not have wanted to live in such a state. From those troubling cases we have descended to the point where last year Jack Kevorkian walked away after assisting in the suicide of a woman who was strong enough to play tennis the day before she died.

A Schizophrenic Attitude

"We have developed a schizophrenic attitude toward persons with disabilities. On the one hand, we are supposed to bring them into the mainstream. On the other, we are being urged to agree that certain disabilities are so severe that killing oneself might be a good idea."

The legal thought opening the door to physician-assisted suicide is not a consistent one. Destro points out that the Second Circuit Court [in a 1996 decision] remained "blissfully ignorant" of (or at least did not recognize) the language in "scores of decisions" that distinguish between "suicide" and the decision to refuse or withdraw useless or unwanted treatment. In this, the court attempted to diminish the scandal of suicide by identifying it with the nonscandalous refusal of heroic treatment.

In mid-1977 there were four major cases pending before the courts (and numerous other ones working their way up) that raise what to Destro is the ultimate question: How important are the lives of disabled people?

"This question brings together Christian notions of the integrity of the person; philosophical notions of what a civilized society is all about; and civil rights notions of equal treatment and equal dignity."

Particularly troubling to Destro, who directs Catholic University's Law and Religion Program, is that the Ninth Circuit Court of Appeals [in a 1996 decision] has taken the position that since individuals are free in a democratic society to keep their religious beliefs to themselves, public policy may reflect only a pro-suicide view. Those who oppose PAS are branded as religious zealots intent on "imposing their morality" on the rest of us.

"It makes one wonder whether Judge Reinhardt dropped in from Mars. Though he claims the authority to sit in judgment of all religiously based moral values, he seems utterly clueless. The very criticisms he levels at opponents of PAS also apply to its champions. If the religious foundations of a law make it suspect, our entire system of civil-rights laws is suspect, too, for it is clearly based on the religious belief that God made us equal."

Destro thus approaches PAS as primarily a civil-rights issue. "If we can't protect people with severe disabilities from those who would 'help' them take their own lives, haven't we assumed the authority to say what a life is worth?"

Destro believes that when the state makes an exception for persons with disabilities, it deprives them of the protection to which they are entitled under homicide laws. At that point, he says, the disabled no longer enjoy "equal protection of the laws." But this removal, tragically enough, is the logical end of where our courts have been heading for some time.

Dangerous Liberty

Such an outcome can be frightening because the limits are so dubious. "Take the Ninth Circuit Court opinion," Destro explains, "which states that 'We hold that a liberty interest exists in the choice of how and when one dies.' We have to ask, to whom does this 'liberty interest' apply? A teenager who wakes up with pimples and who has just been dumped by her boyfriend? Autonomy principles of this type have no logical stopping point."

All this is further complicated by the fact that the definitions of suicide, euthanasia, the disabled, and the terminally ill are too general, too vague, too conflicting, and therefore too dangerous. The result is often ridiculous language, such as when the Ninth Circuit Court extends the "right to die" to persons in an irreversible coma—in which case, of course, it must be exercised by proxy.

As so often happens with judicial activism, when the Ninth Circuit Court judge threw out the Washington State citizens' attempt to ban PAS, he extended the alleged "right" to PAS far beyond what the advocates of PAS dared to advocate. And when people raise concerns about this, they are dismissed as unenlightened.

"There's a cultural snobbery in all of this," Destro points out. "The Ninth Circuit judge treats anybody who has more qualms as a Neanderthal know-nothing."

Where do the conflicting court opinions leave us, legally? Destro's fear is that the Supreme Court will come out [in deciding two right-to-die cases in 1997] with a "wishy washy" opinion that will bring us one step closer to an "open season on the elderly and persons with severe disabilities." While he does not expect the Supreme Court to go as far as the Ninth Circuit Court, if they leave the door open at all, "it will just be a matter of time before the courts find that all the equities favor suicide and euthanasia. The precedents are in place, and their logic is inexorable."

Destro's hope, however, is that people of faith—including Jews, Christians, and Muslims—will view the federal court decisions legalizing euthanasia as a "wake-up call." "These cases are a mirror image of what we have become," says Destro. "Our legal and philosophical elites have lost sight of the reason why we protect minorities and individuals who exist outside the mainstream of society. It is not simply a question of political or economic power. Civil rights is a question of morals."

Working in a Broken System

In the late seventies, Dr. Joanne Lynn was assigned to an "undervalued and academically meaningless job," a nascent hospice program "and a largely ignored nursing home ward full of severely demented and disabled patients in long-term care." She was told that it would be "depressing and medically worthless work." Yet almost 20 years later, and after having served two thousand persons who have died, Lynn describes her work as "wonderful," saying it has been "an extraordinary privilege to have been allowed to travel in the valley of death" with so many patients.

Lynn, a member of the United Church of Christ, points out that one reason that PAS is in such demand is because the level of care among the dying has become so pitiful. "My patients encounter a system that is dominated by concerns adverse to theirs. In our health-care system, it is easier to get open heart surgery than Meals on Wheels and easier to get antibiotics than eyeglasses. If it were easy to get good care, the question of whether one should be able to choose to be killed would be troubling and important. But it is not easy to get good care. In fact, it is so difficult and unlikely that people might well seek death just because doing otherwise is so burdensome."

In the years that Lynn has been involved in caring for the dying, the dynamics of the debate over PAS have changed dramatically. "Ten to fifteen years ago, we were still hotly debating about whether we could stop a ventilator," she laughs. And PAS advocates were considered "way off the far edge."

Lynn believes that one of the social factors that helped change the debate was the emergence of AIDS. Instead of broken and weary 80-year-old citizens dealing with life-threatening diseases and illnesses, affluent 25- to 35-year-old men—eager and able to extend their political clout and organization—suddenly joined the debate. Almost immediately, prolonged deaths became a matter of public discussion.

Lynn approaches the subject of PAS from a perspective that is different from most. The social alienation of the elderly leads her to ask, "We have a care system that does not prioritize pain relief or emotional support—and in this system we want to discuss PAS?

"We deal with so many people for whom their social situation is self-coercive. An 88-year-old lady with bad hearing, bad eyesight, and who has outlived most of her siblings gets a bad disease, doesn't want to be Medicaid dependent, yet doesn't have enough resources and knows she'll end up in a nursing home, which she says she hates." After all this, somewhat understandably, "the patient says she wants to be dead.

"She wouldn't be saying she wants to commit suicide if she had Rockefeller's resources. She's saying she wants to commit suicide because we have made long-term care the step-child of medical care. We've never properly funded long-term care, and we see to it that old people have to be impoverished very near their death." Many elderly people literally face a choice between a friendless and penniless future—a terrifying thought—or death. And they often face this choice in isolation.

It is this elderly, "invisible" patient that concerns Lynn. "For every 60-year-old dying of breast cancer, there's a hundred dying at 85 of uncertain causes. These are the people who should be in the limelight, not the 25-year-old men dying of AIDS."

As a geriatrician, the debate toward PAS in the midst of a broken system puts Lynn in a serious dilemma. "Am I supposed to be willing to be your Nazi doctor treating you as a useless eater, or am I supposed to stand by as society's tormentor and see that these inadequate resources are all you have to live on and that you have to keep living it out?"

Help for the Elderly

According to Lynn, this is the real debate—how we treat or fail to treat the bulk of her elderly, once middle-class patients. Legalized PAS is just one possible solution, one that she believes won't really be the best option for those most likely to be affected by it. "Who will show up when 5 percent of deaths are done this way?" she asks. "It's not going to be the occasional Janet Adkins who can't face the prospect of possibly losing her mind, or the 60-year-old who has just found out he has cancer. It's going to be old people. A 60-year-old still has families, insurance, and people who care. We have an awful lot of 85-year-olds who literally have no one who still cares."

Lynn believes that politicians by and large simply aren't addressing the larger issues. "We're talking about cutting Medicare and our social obligation to take care of the disabled, and at the same time we're also talking about physician-assisted suicide, and no one's noticing that they might come together in a very difficult way. Our society has to learn to debate the issues around these situations. What kind of people are we when we say to the elderly who run into adversity, 'You should just be dead?'"

For solutions, Lynn recommends developing measures that examine the quality of end-of-life care and demanding that certain, agreed-upon standards be met. Popular reports on hospitals—such as *U.S. News and World Report*'s annual issue—don't even mention end-of-life care.

Lynn also views developing a sensible financing system as one of the top priorities. "Right now I can get elegant, $20,000 surgery for a patient at the drop of a hat, but I can't get her lunch. If we were building a system around the fears of 85-year-old women, surely we would make sure they could have lunch!"

The proper treatment of pain is another need that concerns Lynn. She points out emphatically that "no one near death needs to be in pain. People find it hard to believe, but almost all patients can be kept conscious and out of pain. The rest can be kept sedated and out of pain."

Pain goes beyond physical suffering, however, to include emotional isolation. So often, elderly people want to go on living, not just existing. One chaplain told Lynn the story of an elderly, bedridden woman who was dying. Her overly anxious sister attended to her every physical need and persisted to ask the patient if she wanted anything—orange juice, tea, sherbet, ice? Finally, the dying patient took her sister's arm and brought her near so she could hear her speak. "What I really need," the patient told her, "is a tender morsel of juicy gossip."

One of Lynn's nursing-home residents once claimed to find no meaning in life, but gradually grew more at peace. Lynn noticed that she always had her bed cranked up to the same position, so Lynn lay in such a way that she could survey the patient's view, and there she saw a group of large, flowering weeds. That evening, Lynn went out to the yard and brought some of the flowers in and placed them near the patient's dinner tray. Sometimes, a sick patient doesn't really need death, she just needs to be reminded that the outside world still has flowers.

Since, according to Lynn, three-quarters of all people die in federal programs, most medical costs are managed by a bureaucracy. One consequence is that end-of-life care is not cost-effective for most doctors. "If you develop a reputation to be the best in town at providing good end-of-life care, you'll go out of business within a year!" Lynn laughs. "We have to make it possible to have excellence. It has to be possible to be really good at end-of-life care and still be able to make a living. Now, we've perversely set it up so you just can't do it."

Apart from the immorality of PAS, Lynn believes an assisted-suicide law simply is not necessary. Patients already possess the legal authority to give up eating, or to refuse antibiotics or insulin. The only thing a patient now lacks is control over the exact hour of his or her death, making the patient unable to gather family, say good-bye, and then immediately die.

A More Active Role for Religion

Unless someone is willing to underwrite end-of-life care, Lynn suggests that we need to develop an "ethics and a culture" that can deal with these issues—and that means religious bodies need to take a much more active role. "Religious bodies are acting as if the big thing is to comment on physician-assisted suicide. I don't care what they say about physician-assisted suicide. What I want them to do is to say, 'This is what the end of life should look like.' Given our new demographics, how does the church address the old and dying? If a patient can live a little longer with a drug that costs $10,000 a month, should we say yes or should we say no? Do you realize how many people die alone in Washington, D.C.? What does that mean for the church down the block?

"My experience with churches has been fairly grim. If I call up the minister of a church a person attended for 30–40 years in the prime of her life but she's now disabled, and I ask 'Is there anything you can do to help this person's burden?' I'd say I'm no better than 50-50 to get a favorable response—and that's when the doctor is calling!

"Old people getting sick can't count on the church. There is no one to validate the patient's importance. Paid care givers can only go so far.

"If what one faces when one reaches the end of life is being thrown on the dung heap of humanity, then a lot of people are going to choose to be killed—and not foolishly. And then what I am supposed to do?"

Lynn wishes the Christian community would simply become more "thoughtful." "It's not enough to send flowers to shut-ins," she says. Many older people tell Lynn that the only time they ever get touched is during a physical exam. "Why can't we develop hug networks?" she laughs.

"We need to look to find ways to validate the humanity of people who are getting near the end of their lives. Take the last 20 members who have died in your congregation and ask their families how the church responded. I've had patients who were furious when they received cards telling them people were praying for them. 'Well, why don't they come and meet me?' they ask. 'Why won't they pray with me in person while holding my hand?'"

THERE IS LITTLE DIFFERENCE BETWEEN ACTIVE AND PASSIVE EUTHANASIA

Roger J. Miner

In rendering the decision of the U.S. Court of Appeals for the Second Circuit in the case of *Quill v. New York State Attorney General* on April 2, 1996, Judge Roger J. Miner states that he sees no real distinction between discontinuing life-sustaining treatment and providing drugs for suicide at a terminally ill patient's request. In June 1997 the Supreme Court rejected Miner's claim that the Constitution therefore protects the right to assisted suicide. Many supporters of assisted suicide, however, accept Miner's view from an ethical standpoint. Miner is Adjunct Professor of Law at Albany Law School of Union University (New York) as well as a circuit court judge.

According to the Fourteenth Amendment, the equal protection of the laws cannot be denied by any State to any person within its jurisdiction. This constitutional guarantee simply requires the states to treat in a similar manner all individuals who are similarly situated. But disparate treatment is not necessarily a denial of the equal protection guaranteed by the Constitution. The Supreme Court has described the wide discretion afforded to the states in establishing acceptable classifications:

> The Equal Protection Clause directs that "all persons similarly circumstanced shall be treated alike." But so too, "[t]he Constitution does not require things which are different in fact or opinion to be treated in law as though they were the same." The initial discretion to determine what is "different" and what is "the same" resides in the legislatures of the States. A legislature must have substantial latitude to establish classifications that roughly approximate the nature of the problem perceived, that accommodate competing concerns both public and private, and that account for limitations on the practical ability of the State to remedy every ill. In applying the Equal Projection Clause to most forms of state action, we thus

Excerpted from opinion of Roger J. Miner, U.S. Court of Appeals for the Second Circuit, April 2, 1996, in *Quill v. New York State Attorney General*.

seek only the assurance that the classification at issue bears some fair relationship to a legitimate public purpose.

. . . Applying the foregoing principles to the New York statutes criminalizing assisted suicide, it seems clear that: 1) the statutes in question fall within the category of social welfare legislation and therefore are subject to rational basis scrutiny upon judicial review; 2) New York law does not treat equally all competent persons who are in the final stages of fatal illness and wish to hasten their deaths; 3) the distinctions made by New York law with regard to such persons do not further any legitimate state purpose; and 4) accordingly, to the extent that the statutes in question prohibit persons in the final stages of terminal illness from having assistance in ending their lives by the use of self-administered, prescribed drugs, the statutes lack any rational basis and are violative of the Equal Protection Clause.

Right to Refuse Treatment

The right to refuse medical treatment long has been recognized in New York. In 1914 Judge Cardozo wrote that, under New York law, "[e]very human being of adult years and sound mind has a right to determine what shall be done with his own body." In 1981, the New York Court of Appeals held that this right extended to the withdrawal of life-support systems. The *Eichner* case involved a terminally-ill, 83-year-old patient whose guardian ultimately was authorized to withdraw the patient's respirator. The [New York] Court of Appeals determined that the guardian had proved by clear and convincing evidence that the patient, prior to becoming incompetent due to illness, had consistently expressed his view that life should not be prolonged if there was no hope of recovery. In *Stonar,* the companion case to *Eichner,* the Court of Appeals determined that a profoundly retarded, terminally-ill patient was incapable of making a decision to terminate blood transfusions. There, the patient was incapable of making a reasoned decision, having never been competent at any time in his life. In both these cases, the New York Court of Appeals recognized the right of a competent, terminally-ill patient to hasten his death upon proper proof of his desire to do so.

The [New York] Court of Appeals revisited the issue in *Rivers v. Katz.* In that case, the Court recognized the right to bring on death by refusing medical treatment not only as a "fundamental common-law right" but also as "coextensive with [a] patient's liberty interest protected by the due process clause of our State Constitution." The following language was included in the opinion:

> In our system of a free government, where notions of individual autonomy and free choice are cherished, it is the individual who must have the final say in respect to decisions regarding his medical treatment in order to insure that the

greatest possible protection is accorded his autonomy and freedom from unwanted interference with the furtherance of his own desires.

After these cases were decided, the [legislature] placed its imprimatur upon the right of competent citizens to hasten death by refusing medical treatment and by directing physicians to remove life-support systems already in place. In 1987, the legislature enacted Article 29-B of the New York Public Health Law, entitled "Orders Not to Resuscitate." The Article provides that an "adult with capacity" may direct the issuance of an order not to resuscitate. . . .

In 1990, the New York legislature enacted Article 29-C of the Public Health Law, entitled "Health Care Agents and Proxies." This statute allows for a person to sign a health care proxy, for the purpose of appointing an agent with "authority to make any and all health care decisions on the principal's behalf that the principal could make." These decisions include those relating to the administration of artificial nutrition and hydration, provided the wishes of the principal are known to the agent. . . .

The Cruzan Case

The concept that a competent person may order the removal of life-support systems found [U.S.] Supreme Court approval in *Cruzan* [a 1990 decision]. . . . There the Court upheld a determination of the Missouri Supreme Court that required proof by clear and convincing evidence of a patient's desire for the withdrawal of life-sustaining equipment. The patient in that case, Nancy Cruzan, was in a persistent vegetative state as the result of injuries sustained in an automobile accident. Her parents sought court approval in the State of Missouri to terminate the artificial nutrition and hydration with which she was supplied at the state hospital where she was confined. The hospital employees refused to withdraw the life-support systems, without which Cruzan would suffer certain death. The trial court authorized the withdrawal after finding that Cruzan had expressed some years before to a housemate friend some thoughts that suggested she would not wish to live on a life-support system. The trial court also found that one in Cruzan's condition had a fundamental right to refuse death-prolonging procedures.

The Missouri Supreme Court, in reversing the trial court, refused to find a broad right of privacy in the state constitution that would support a right to refuse treatment. Moreover, that court doubted that such a right existed under the United States Constitution. It did identify a state policy in the Missouri Living Will Statute favoring the preservation of life and concluded that, in the absence of compliance with the statute's formalities or clear and convincing evidence of the patient's choice, no person could order the withdrawal of medical life-support services.

In affirming the Missouri Supreme Court, the United States Supreme Court stated: "The principle that a competent person has a constitutionally protected liberty interest in refusing unwanted medical treatment may be inferred from our prior decisions." The Court noted that the inquiry is not ended by the identification of a liberty interest, because there also must be a balancing of the state interests and the individual's liberty interests before there can be a determination that constitutional rights have been violated. The Court all but made that determination in the course of the following analysis:

> Petitioners insist that under the general holdings of our cases, the forced administration of life-sustaining medical treatment, and even of artificially-delivered food and water essential to life, would implicate a competent person's liberty interest. Although we think the logic of the cases discussed above would embrace such a liberty interest, the dramatic consequences involved in refusal of such treatment would inform the inquiry as to whether the deprivation of that interest is constitutionally permissible. But for purposes of this case, we assume that the United States Constitution would grant a competent person a constitutionally protected right to refuse lifesaving hydration and nutrition.

The Court went on to find that Missouri allowed a surrogate to "act for the patient in electing to have hydration and nutrition withdrawn in such a way as to cause death," subject to "a procedural safeguard to assure that the action of the surrogate conforms as best it may to the wishes expressed by the patient while competent." The Court then held that the procedural safeguard or requirement imposed by Missouri—the heightened evidentiary requirement that the incompetent's wishes be proved by clear and convincing evidence—was not forbidden by the United States Constitution.

Unequal Treatment

In view of the foregoing, it seems clear that New York does not treat similarly circumstanced persons alike: those in the final stages of terminal illness who are on life-support systems are allowed to hasten their deaths by directing the removal of such systems; but those who are similarly situated, except for the previous attachment of life-sustaining equipment, are not allowed to hasten death by self-administering prescribed drugs. The district judge [ruling on this case] has identified "a difference between allowing nature to take its course, even in the most severe situations, and intentionally using an artificial death-producing device." But Justice Scalia, for one, has remarked upon "the irrelevance of the action-inaction distinction," noting that "the cause of death in both cases is the suicide's conscious decision to 'pu[t] an end to his own existence.'"

Indeed, there is nothing "natural" about causing death by means other than the original illness or its complications. The withdrawal of nutrition brings on death by starvation, the withdrawal of hydration [fluids] brings on death by dehydration, and the withdrawal of ventilation brings about respiratory failure. By ordering the discontinuance of these artificial life-sustaining processes or refusing to accept them in the first place, a patient hastens his death by means that are not natural in any sense. It certainly cannot be said that the death that immediately ensues is the natural result of the progression of the disease or condition from which the patient suffers.

Moreover, the writing of a prescription to hasten death, after consultation with a patient, involves a far less active role for the physician than is required in bringing about death through asphyxiation [deprivation of oxygen], starvation and/or dehydration. Withdrawal of life support requires physicians or those acting at their direction physically to remove equipment and, often, to administer palliative drugs which may themselves contribute to death. The ending of life by these means is nothing more nor less than assisted suicide. It simply cannot be said that those mentally competent, terminally-ill persons who seek to hasten death but whose treatment does not include life support are treated equally.

Competing State Interests

A finding of unequal treatment does not, of course, end the inquiry, unless it is determined that the inequality is not rationally related to some legitimate state interest. The burden is upon the [doctors] to demonstrate irrationality. At oral argument and in its brief, the state's contention has been that its principal interest is in preserving the life of all its citizens at all times and under all conditions. But what interest can the state possibly have in requiring the prolongation of a life that is all but ended? Surely, the state's interest lessens as the potential for life diminishes. And what business is it of the state to require the continuation of agony when the result is imminent and inevitable? What concern prompts the state to interfere with a mentally competent patient's "right to define [his] own concept of existence, of meaning, of the universe, and of the mystery of human life," when the patient seeks to have drugs prescribed to end life during the final stages of a terminal illness? The greatly reduced interest of the state in preserving life compels the answer to these questions: "None."

In 1996 a panel of the Ninth Circuit attempted to identify some state interests in reversing a district court decision holding unconstitutional a statute of the State of Washington criminalizing the promotion of a suicide attempt. The plaintiffs in the Washington case contended for physician-assisted suicide for the terminally-ill, but the panel majority found that the statute prohibiting suicide promotion furthered the following: the interest in denying to physicians "the role of killers of their patients"; the interest in avoiding psychological pressure upon the elderly and infirm to consent to death; the interest of preventing the exploitation of the poor and minorities; the interest in protecting handicapped persons against societal indifference; the interest in preventing the sort of abuse that "has occurred in the Netherlands where . . . legal guidelines have tacitly allowed assisted suicide or euthanasia in response to a repeated request from a suffering, competent patient." The panel majority also raised a question relative to the lack of clear definition of the term "terminally ill."

State Interests Are Not Served

The New York statutes prohibiting assisted suicide, which are similar to the Washington statute, do not serve any of the state interests noted, in view of the statutory and common law schemes allowing suicide through the withdrawal of life-sustaining treatment. Physicians do not fulfill the role of "killer" by prescribing drugs to hasten death any more than they do by disconnecting life-support systems. Likewise, "psychological pressure" can be applied just as much upon the elderly and infirm to consent to withdrawal of life-sustaining equipment as to take drugs to hasten death.

There is no clear indication that there has been any problem in regard to the former, and there should be none as to the latter. In any event, the state of New York may establish rules and procedures to assure that all choices are free of such pressures. With respect to the protection of minorities, the poor and the non-mentally handicapped, it suffices to say that these classes of persons are entitled to treatment equal to that afforded to all those who now may hasten death by means of life-support withdrawal. In point of fact, these persons *themselves* are entitled to hasten death by requesting such withdrawal and should be free to do so by requesting appropriate medication to terminate life during the final stages of terminal illness.

As to the interest in avoiding abuse similar to that occurring in the Netherlands, it seems clear that some physicians there practice nonvoluntary euthanasia, although it is not legal to do so. The [doctors] here do not argue for euthanasia at all but for assisted suicide for terminally-ill, mentally competent patients, who would self-administer the lethal drugs. It is difficult to see how the relief the [doctors] seek would lead to the abuses found in the Netherlands. Moreover, note should be taken of the fact that in 1993 the Royal Dutch Medical Association adopted new guidelines for those physicians who choose to accede to the wishes of patients to hasten death. Under the new guidelines, patients must self-administer drugs whenever possible, and physicians must obtain a second opinion from another physician who has no relationship with the requesting physician or his patient.

Finally, it seems clear that most physicians would agree on the definition of "terminally ill," at least for the purpose of the relief that [the doctors] seek. The [doctors] seek to hasten death only where a patient is in the "final stages" of "terminal illness," and it seems even more certain that physicians would agree on when this condition occurs. Physicians are accustomed to advising patients and their families in this regard and frequently do so when decisions are to be made regarding the furnishing or withdrawal of life-support systems. Again, New York may define that stage of illness with greater particularity, require the opinion of more than one physician or impose any other obligation upon patients and physicians who collaborate in hastening death.

The New York statutes criminalizing assisted suicide violate the Equal Protection Clause because, to the extent that they prohibit a physician from prescribing medications to be self-administered by a mentally competent, terminally-ill person in the final stages of his terminal illness, they are not rationally related to any legitimate state interest.

We reverse the judgment of the district court. . . .

THE DISTINCTION BETWEEN KILLING AND LETTING DIE IS ESSENTIAL

John J. Paris

John J. Paris, a member of the Society of Jesus (the Jesuit order of priests) and Walsh Professor of Bioethics at Boston College, maintains that the distinction between active euthanasia (or assisting in suicide) and passive euthanasia (ending life-supporting medical treatment) is a very important one in terms of medical ethics. Paris sees it as the difference between killing and letting die. Nonetheless, he writes, this distinction has been obscured by an excessive emphasis on autonomy, or independence in decision-making.

The morality of suicide is not the subject of the public policy debate. What is new is the desire to medicalize suicide and active euthanasia.

> To die proudly when it is no longer possible to live proudly. Death freely chosen, death at the right time, brightly and cheerfully accomplished amid children and witnesses. . . . From love of life, one should desire a different death: free, conscious, without accident, without ambush.
>
> —Friedrich Nietzsche

Constitutional analysis and legal reasoning cannot and will not settle the ongoing debate over physician-assisted death. Answers to such fundamental questions as the meaning and purpose of life are not derived from judicial precedents nor judges' decrees. . . .

The morality of suicide itself is not the subject of the public policy debate. What is new in our era is the desire to medicalize suicide and active euthanasia. We want physicians to provide the means to end one's life in an antiseptically acceptable fashion. Suicide by knives, guns, ropes and bridges tends to be messy. We seek a more aesthetically pleasing way of ending life.

A Search for Control over Dying

What led to this situation, one so fundamentally at odds with the 2,500-year old Hippocratic tradition that the physician as healer was

From "Autonomy and Physician-Assisted Suicide," by John J. Paris, *America*, May 17, 1997. Reprinted with permission of America Press, Inc., www.americapress.org. Copyright © 1997. All Rights Reserved.

never to administer a lethal potion? In great part today's demands are a result of medicine's successes. We have come to believe that the "miracles" of modern medicine are able not only to defeat disease but to conquer death. With the rise of technological medicine, lives that once were beyond rescue can now be saved. Sometimes, however, that success comes at too great a price: a life of suffering, pain and despair. Patients [in comas] like Karen Ann Quinlan or Nancy Cruzan may now lie trapped by a halfway technology, one that can ward off death but not restore health, in a situation worse than death itself—an endless prolongation of their dying.

Once the quest for salvation through science and immortality through medicine proves unavailing, we seek a different medical "fix" for our problem. Since we fear death and the unrelieved suffering that prolonged dying can produce, we turn to medicine for relief from both. Commenting on that issue, Daniel Callahan, president of the Hastings Center, writes in "Aid-in-Dying," a 1991 article in *Commonweal*, that the movement to legalize euthanasia and assisted suicide is a "historically inevitable response to that fear." He traces that response to what the late Cardinal Joseph Bernardin described as the "increasingly mechanistic, commercial and soulless" process of modern medicine. Caring, which traditionally characterized the profession, is now being pushed aside for profit. In such an environment it is not surprising that Jack Kevorkian is held up as the model of a "good doctor."

Dr. Kevorkian, as George Annas, the Utley Professor of Health Law at Boston University's School of Public Health, puts it, is not simply an aberrant physician; he is "a symptom of a medical care system gone seriously wrong at the end of life." It is a system that treats death not as an integral part of nature, like birth and life itself, but as "an offense against nature"—something to be fought off at all cost or, if that battle is not successful, to be slain.

The inability of modern medicine to reassure us that it can manage our dying with dignity and comfort is documented by the SUPPORT [the Study to Understand Prognoses and Preferences for Outcomes and Risks of Treatment] finding reported in the *Journal of the American Medical Association* in 1995. Half of all conscious patients who died in the hospital, it was found, experienced moderate to severe pain at least half the time during their last three days of life. This leads to the demand that we be allowed to take back control of our fate. In face of this powerful, almost relentless dynamic, Callahan asks how do we accomplish that goal. He observes that "for many the answer seems obvious and unavoidable, that of active euthanasia and assisted suicide."

The 1991 referendum in Washington State was the first public attempt to achieve that end. Though defeated in a close vote, that referendum set the stage for the successful ballot measure three years later in Oregon, by which, for the first time in our nation's history, voters sanctioned state approval of physician-assisted suicide. The outcome in Oregon was not surprising. Public opinion polls in this country consistently show that 65 percent of the populace support such a proposition. In great part that support is a reflection of two cultural phenomena that have emerged and flourished over the last 25 years: an emphasis on individual autonomy and the transformation of American medicine from a caring profession into a business designed to serve demands for medical services.

One of the striking features of this shift was the triumph of the patient "rights" movement over against the long-standing tradition of medical paternalism. The corollary of the emphasis on patient autonomy was the obligation of medicine to respond to patient desires. The legislative response to that emphasis was the Patient Self-Determination Act of 1990 (P.S.D.A.), in which Congress mandated that health care facilities must inform patients of their right to decline any unwanted medical treatment, including those that are potentially life-prolonging.

In enacting P.S.D.A. the Congress was in accord with 400 years of consistent Catholic moral teaching that no one is obliged to undergo a proposed medical treatment that is disproportionately painful or burdensome. That doctrine is best summed up, in the Vatican's 1980 *Declaration on Euthanasia*, in which we read:

> [O]ne cannot impose on anyone the obligation to have recourse to a technique which is already in use but which carries a risk or is burdensome. Such a refusal is not the equivalent of suicide (or euthanasia); on the contrary, it should be considered as an acceptance of the human condition, or a wish to avoid the application of a medical procedure disproportionate to the results that can be expected.

That declaration, however, makes a sharp distinction between refusing measures that would serve "only [to sustain] a precarious and burdensome prolongation of life" and suicide or active euthanasia. The former is permitted the latter is prohibited.

Killing and Letting Die

The word euthanasia ("good death") is subject to widely differing understandings, and the distinction between active and passive euthanasia (killing and letting die) is frequently collapsed into the one term. The now famous essay "Active and Passive Euthanasia," by James Rachaels, professor of bioethics at Monash University in Melbourne, Australia, which appeared in the *New England Journal of Medicine* in 1975, denies any real difference between the two. For him, "if a doctor lets a patient die, for humane reasons, he is in the same moral position as if he had given the patient a lethal injection."

The supporters of unlimited patient autonomy agree. They place no constraint and no limitation on an individual's autonomous "right" to direct medical treatment. The patient alone determines not only what medical intervention will be undergone, but whether medicine should be enlisted in the ending of life itself. The highly publicized Philosophers' Brief to the Supreme Court in a physician-assisted suicide case in 1997 starkly puts it thus: "If it is permissible for a doctor deliberately to withdraw medical treatment in order to allow death to result from a natural process, then it is equally permissible for him to help a patient hasten his own death more actively, if that is the patient's express wish."

That brief, as well as the rulings of several Federal courts in cases of physician-assisted suicide in 1996, rejects any distinction between killing and letting die. As Dworkin put it in a commentary on the oral argument at the Supreme Court on Jan. 8, 1997, in the physician-assisted suicide case: "One Justice suggested that a patient who insists that life support be disconnected is not committing suicide. That's wrong: he is committing suicide if he aims at death, as most such patients do. Just as someone whose wrist is cut in an accident is committing suicide if he refuses to try to stop the bleeding."

If that thesis is correct, we land in one of two seemingly untenable positions: If killing is seen as morally wrong, then we cannot withdraw life-prolonging medical procedures that are overly burdensome to the patient. That was the argument made by the trial court in the Quinlan case, in which Judge Robert Muir ruled that removing the ventilator would subject the physicians to charges of homicide. Such rulings, which allow "no exit" from medical technology, exemplify Sartre's definition of hell. They also lead to cries for relief, including demands for active euthanasia.

Alternatively, if there is no distinction between killing and letting die, and if one holds, as do all the courts of final jurisdiction that have addressed the issue, that it is morally and legally acceptable to withhold or withdraw unwanted medical interventions, then there is no barrier to "killing" the patient. As Rachaels puts it, the physician is in the same moral position "if he [gives] the patient a lethal injection as in withdrawing a respirator." In fact, Rachaels argued that since the latter action spares the patient from suffering, it is "actually preferable."

To avoid confusion in this debate, it is imperative to have a clear definition of terms. Here euthanasia is defined as "the deliberate action by a physician to terminate the life of a patient." The clearest example is the act of lethal injection. Singer and Siegler's essay "Euthanasia—a Critique," in the *New England Journal of Medicine* (1991), provides the helpful distinction between that action and such other acts as the decision to forego life-sustaining treatment (including the use of ventilation, cardio-pulmonary resuscitation, dialysis or tube feedings); or the administration of analgesic agents to relieve pain; or "assisted suicide" in which the doctor prescribes but does not administer a lethal dose of medication; or "mercy killing" performed by a patient's family or friends.

Denying Traditions

Catholic tradition, as the Vatican declaration makes clear, opposes euthanasia, or the direct intentional killing of innocent life, whether of "a fetus or an embryo, an infant or an adult, an old person, or one suffering from an incurable disease, or a person who is dying." Furthermore, the church holds that "no one is permitted to ask for this act of killing for himself or herself," nor is it morally licit to consent to such an action for one entrusted to your care. The reason for these moral imperatives is found in the declaration's statement: "Only the Creator of life has the right to take away the life of the innocent." To arrogate that right to ourselves, whether as patient, guardian or caregiver would be a "violation of the divine law" and "an offense against the dignity of the human person."

Referendums, legislative enactments or judicial approval of state sanctioned physician assistance in death stand as a challenge to that tradition. What is being asked for in these movements is most clearly seen in the Washington State referendum, in which voters were asked to approve what its proponents labeled "a new medical service"— namely, authorization for physicians actively to assist a terminally ill patient to die. The ballot initiative was circulated with the title, "Shall adult patients who are in a medically terminal condition be permitted to request and receive from a physician aid-in-dying?" The reality beneath that innocuously worded heading was that "aid-in-dying" meant "aid in the form of a medical service, provided in person by a physician, that will end the life of a conscious and mentally qualified patient in a dignified, painless, and humane manner, when requested voluntarily by the patient through a written directive . . . at the time the medical service is to be provided."

From the time of Hippocrates through the 1997 *Current Opinions of the American Medical Association's Council on Ethical and Judicial Affairs*, Western medicine has regarded the killing of patients, even on request, as a profound violation of the deepest meaning of the medical vocation. Leon Kass, professor of humanities at the University of Chicago, undertook to explain the reasons for the societal change on this question in a deeply probing 1989 essay in *The Public Interest* entitled "Why Doctors Must Not Kill." There he argued that the basis for the shift in attitude, which has already led to some 5,000 cases of active euthanasia or assisted suicide a year in the Netherlands, is an overemphasis on freedom and personal autonomy, expressed in the view that each one has a right to control his or her body and life, including the end of it. In this view, physicians are bound to acquiesce not only to demands for termination of treatment, but also to intentional killing through poison, because the right to choose—freedom—

must be respected even more than life itself. The second reason advanced for killing patients is not a concern for choice, but the assessment by the patient or others that the patient's life is no longer deemed worth living. It is not autonomy but the miserable or pitiable condition of the body or mind that warrants, in Kass's words, "doing the patient in."

Honoring a Divine Gift

Both of these positions—an absolutizing of individual autonomy and the belief that a life so devoid of dignity should be destroyed—run counter to the Catholic understanding of life as a divine gift over which we exercise stewardship, not dominion. Rather than the complete control over life demanded by the Philosophers' Brief, according to which life is to be ended when we conclude that living on "would disfigure rather than enhance the lives we have created," the Christian finds death's meaning in the example of the suffering Savior who abandoned himself in perfect obedience to the Father's will.

The recent example of Cardinal Joseph Bernardin's very public dying, which *Newsweek* captured in a 1996 cover story, "Teaching Us How to Die," stands in sharp contrast to the view that control and domination over death is the goal. As Cardinal Bernardin expressed it in his parting legacy, *The Gift of Peace*: "I now realize that when I asked my doctor for the test results [which showed metastatic cancer], I had to let go of everything. God was teaching me how little control we really have." His conclusion when he understood that he was dying was uncomplicated: God "is now calling me home."

Self-abandonment to the will of God, not self-determination or the triumph of the human will, is the Christian response when medicine is unable to reverse the dying process. This is because in the Christian tradition death is not the final victor; it is, rather, a "transition from earthly life to life eternal." That truth is movingly set forth in the final movement of Mahler's *"Resurrection" Symphony*, in which amidst the soaring music we hear words of hope in the face of death:

> I am from God and to God I shall return!
> Rise up, yes you will rise up,
> My heart, in an instant!
> What you have conquered
> Shall lead you to God.

The message of the triumph of Christ's resurrection over death, which Mahler heard at a friend's funeral, led him from despair at the friend's death to hope, a hope expressed in the glorious finale of his symphony. It is also the counter-point to the belief that death is something we freely choose "when it is no longer possible to live proudly."

GLOSSARY

active euthanasia Taking a deliberate action, such as injecting a lethal drug, to end a person's life for the purpose of relieving suffering. Compare to **passive euthanasia**.

advance directive Any of several types of legal documents that competent adults may use to state their wishes about health care decisions to be made on their behalf if they become incompetent.

Alzheimer's disease An incurable disease that causes slow destruction of the brain, with loss of memory and mental functions. It usually strikes the elderly.

amyotrophic lateral sclerosis (ALS) An incurable disease of unknown cause in which the nerves that control movement slowly break down, leaving a person increasingly paralyzed. Sometimes called **Lou Gehrig's disease**.

antidepressant A medication, such as Prozac, prescribed to treat depression.

assisted death Any form of hastening a person's death, at his or her request, for the purpose of ending suffering, including physician-assisted suicide, euthanasia (in its narrower meaning), and, possibly, ending of life-sustaining medical treatment. Same as euthanasia in its broader meaning.

autonomy Self-determination or independence; the right to control and make decisions about one's own life.

controlled substances Drugs that are often abused, such as narcotics. Their availability is limited by special laws such as the Controlled Substances Act.

Death with Dignity Act A law in Oregon that legalizes physician-assisted suicide for terminally ill people under certain conditions. The law was passed by voters in November 1994, but court challenges prevented it from going into effect until October 1997.

dementia A breakdown of mental functions, including memory and judgment.

dialysis Filtering of the blood to remove harmful substances, given to people whose kidneys (which normally do this job) are not functioning.

double effect Refers to an action that has an intended good effect and also a bad effect that can be predicted but is not desired. An example is a physician giving a terminally ill person in pain a high dose of narcotics for the intended purpose of controlling the pain, knowing that the drugs may have the second, unintended effect of shortening or even ending the person's life. See also **terminal sedation**.

Down syndrome A group of birth defects that includes moderate to severe learning disability (developmental disability) and various physical problems.

Drug Enforcement Administration (DEA) The agency of the U.S. government responsible for enforcing federal laws that control dangerous drugs such as narcotics.

durable power of attorney for health care A legal document in which competent adults appoint another person (a surrogate) to make health care decisions for them if they should become incompetent. It is also known as a health care proxy and is one form of advance directive.

euthanasia Ending a person's life in order to relieve suffering. Euthanasia sometimes refers to any method of hastening a suffering person's death, including ending life-sustaining medical treatment, assisting in suicide, and taking direct action (such as giving a lethal injection) to cause death. At other times, it refers only to taking direct action to cause another's death.

geriatrician A physician who specializes in treating the elderly.

Hippocratic Oath An oath supposed to have been written by the Greek physician Hippocrates, who lived during the fourth century B.C. It is still considered a major statement of medical ethics, and physicians often recite it when graduating from medical school. It includes a promise to "give no deadly drug, even when asked for it."

hospice An institution or program that offers physical, psychological, and spiritual comfort to dying people and their families.

hydration Giving a person water or other liquids to sustain life.

ICU Abbreviation for Intensive Care Unit, a part of a hospital in which extremely sick patients are cared for.

involuntary euthanasia Killing a competent person (one able to make decisions about his or her medical treatment) for the purpose of relieving suffering without first obtaining the person's permission.

living will A legal document in which a competent adult specifies medical treatments to be given or withheld if he or she becomes incompetent. It may also describe conditions under which the person wants all treatment stopped. A living will is one form of advance directive.

Lou Gehrig's disease Another name for amyotrophic lateral sclerosis, referring to a famous baseball player who suffered from the disease.

nonvoluntary euthanasia Euthanasia of an incompetent person (one unable to make decisions about his or her medical treatment) at the request of a third party.

obitiatrist A word coined by Jack Kevorkian, referring to a physician who specializes in hastening death for patients who request it.

oncology The study and treatment of cancer.

Pain Relief Promotion Act A proposed federal law that would make it illegal for physicians to prescribe controlled substances for the purpose of suicide, thus more or less voiding Oregon's Death with Dignity Act. The House of Representatives passed this bill in October 1999, but it was blocked in the Senate in December 2000.

palliative care Care that gives comfort to dying or incurably ill people and their families but does not attempt to cure disease. It usually includes psychological and spiritual counseling as well as relief of unpleasant physical effects such as pain and nausea.

passive euthanasia Refraining from or stopping an action, such as life-sustaining medical treatment, in order to let a terminally ill person die naturally.

Patient Self-Determination Act An act passed by Congress in November 1990 that requires all health care institutions receiving federal funding to inform patients about their rights to fill out advance directives and refuse medical treatment.

persistent vegetative state A deep and usually permanent state of unawareness, caused by damage to the higher brain. Sometimes popularly called a coma.

physician-assisted suicide An act in which a physician provides the means for suicide, usually a prescription for a lethal dose of drugs, to someone who is terminally or incurably ill. The patient must take the final action that causes his or her death, such as swallowing the drugs.

prognosis Prediction of the outcome of a disease or medical condition in a particular patient.

secobarbital (Seconal) A powerful narcotic, often considered the drug of choice for physician-assisted suicide.

slippery slope argument Ethical argument based on the idea that certain acts, although not morally wrong in themselves, unavoidably lead to other acts that are wrong. For right-to-die opponents, this argument means that social or legal acceptance of each stage of aid in dying (refusal of life-sustaining treatment, physician-assisted suicide, voluntary euthanasia) is bound to lead to the next stage, eventually resulting in euthanasia committed against a person's will. The argument can also refer to broadening of the categories of people who are eligible for aid in dying, beginning with terminally ill, competent adults and ending with competent elderly or disabled people who have not given their consent.

symptom Sign or feature of a disease or medical condition, such as pain or nausea.

terminal illness An illness expected to cause death in a short time, usually within six months.

terminal sedation Giving a terminally ill person a dose of narcotics, in order to relieve pain or other symptoms, that is high enough to make the person deeply unconscious. Death soon results from suppression of breathing, the underlying disease, or lack of food and water. Sometimes called **double effect**.

voluntary active euthanasia Killing a person at the person's request for the purpose of relieving the person's suffering from a terminal or incurable illness or injury.

ORGANIZATIONS TO CONTACT

The editors have compiled the following list of organizations concerned with the issues presented in this book. The descriptions are derived from materials provided by the organizations. All have publications or information available for interested readers. The list was compiled on the date of publication of the present volume; the information provided here may change. Be aware that many organizations take several weeks or longer to respond to inquiries, so allow as much time as possible.

American Foundation for Suicide Prevention
120 Wall St., 22nd Floor, New York, NY 10005
(888) 333-2377 • fax: (212) 363-6237
e-mail: inquiry@afsp.org • website: www.afsp.org

This group, whose medical director is psychiatrist Herbert Hendin, supports research and education on depression and suicide. It opposes legalization of physician-assisted suicide. Its website offers a policy statement giving reasons for its stand on this issue.

American Life League
P.O. Box 1350, Stafford, VA 22555
(540) 659-4171 • fax: (540) 259-6586
e-mail: jsweinberg@all.org • website: www.all.org

This group believes that all human life is sacred and works to build a society that respects and protects human life from fertilization to natural death. It opposes legalization of euthanasia and physician-assisted suicide. Material on these subjects can be found on its website under "Life Issues." This material includes discussions of Jack Kevorkian and the Pain Relief Promotion Act.

American Society of Law, Medicine, and Ethics
765 Commonwealth Avenue, Suite 1634, Boston, MA 02215
(617) 262-4990 • fax: (617) 437-7596
e-mail: info@aslme.org • website: www.aslme.org

This group acts as a forum for discussion of issues including euthanasia and physician-assisted suicide. Its material is aimed primarily at professionals in the fields of health care and law. It publishes two quarterly journals, *Journal of Law, Medicine, and Ethics* and *American Journal of Law and Medicine.* Its website includes a number of papers on assisted suicide, pain relief, and end-of-life care, such as "Guidelines for Physician-Assisted Suicide: Can the Challenge Be Met?"

Americans for Better Care of the Dying
4125 Albemarle St., NW, Suite 210, Washington, DC 20016
(202) 895-9485 • fax: (202) 895-9484
e-mail: info@abcd-caring.org • website: www.abcd-caring.org

This organization, headed by geriatrician Joanne Lynn, is dedicated to social, professional, and policy reform that will improve the care system for patients with serious or terminal illnesses. It emphasizes improved palliative care as an alternative to physician-assisted suicide. It offers action guides for citizens, physicians, and others as well as two books, *Handbook for Mortals* and *Improving Care at the End of Life.*

Citizens United Resisting Euthanasia, Ltd. (CURE)
812 Stephen St., Berkeley Springs, WV 25411
(304) 258-5433 • fax: (304) 258-5420
e-mail: cureltd@ix.netcom.com
website: pweb.netcom.com/~cureltd/index.html

CURE, Ltd. is a grassroots organization that defends the rights of patients to receive medical treatment under all circumstances. It opposes euthanasia without compromise or exception. Its website contains numerous papers, including "Life Matters Brochures," "Living Will—No! Will to Live—Yes!" and "Prenatal Euthanasia—Genetic Genocide."

Compassion in Dying Federation
PMB 415, 6312 SW Capitol Hwy., Portland, OR 97201
(503) 221-9556 • fax: (503) 228-9160
e-mail: info@CompassionInDying.org • website: www.CompassionInDying.org

This group provides client service, legal advocacy, and public education to improve management of pain and other physical problems and increase patient self-determination. It favors expanding end-of-life choices to include aid in dying for terminally ill, mentally competent adults. It publishes a newsletter, available online, at irregular intervals. It also has press releases online, such as "CID-led coalition petitions Health Care Financing Administration for action on pain care policy."

Death with Dignity National Center
11 Dupont Circle NW, Suite 202, Washington, DC 20036
(202) 969-1669 • fax: (202) 969-1668
e-mail: info@deathwithdignity.org • website: www.deathwithdignity.org

This organization promotes a comprehensive, humane system of care for terminally ill patients. It works to increase patients' choices and autonomy, including choices to hasten death. Its website includes a glossary, a timeline of events related to physician aid in dying, links, articles, and international news briefs on this subject.

Dying with Dignity
55 Eglinton Ave. East, Suite 705, Toronto ON M4P 1G8, Canada
(800) 495-6156 • fax: (416) 489-9010
e-mail: dwdca@web.net • website: www.web.net/dwd/

This Canadian society is concerned with the quality of dying. It advises patients about their right to choose health care options at the end of life, distributes advance directives, and works for legal changes to permit voluntary, physician-assisted dying. Dying with Dignity publishes a quarterly newsletter, available online. Its website also includes other material related to assisted dying, such as a poll of Canadians' opinions on the subject.

Euthanasia Prevention Coalition BC
103-2609 Westview Dr., Suite 126, North Vancouver, BC V7N 4N2, Canada
(604) 794-3772 • fax: (604) 794-3960
e-mail: info@epc.bc.ca • website: www.epc.bc.ca

This coalition, headquartered in British Columbia, Canada, opposes legalization or promotion of euthanasia and physician-assisted suicide. It educates the public about the risks of these activities and advises on alternative methods of relieving suffering. Its website includes briefs to the Canadian legislature, commentaries, news items, and press releases such as "Laws Against Euthanasia

Protect Us All" (commentary). It also publishes a newsletter and a video, "Who Gets . . . The Last Word?"

Euthanasia Research and Guidance Organization (ERGO)
24829 Norris Ln., Junction City, OR 97448-9559
(541) 998-1873 • fax: (541) 998-1873
e-mail: ergo@efn.org • website: www.finalexit.org

ERGO advises terminally ill people and their families about hastened death through literature and online material. It supports choice and, if necessary, help in dying for those who desire it. Its website includes a glossary, chronology, news stories and other resources related to the right-to-die movement. It sells books by right-to-die proponent Derek Humphry and others, such as *Final Exit* and *The Right to Die: Understanding Euthanasia.*

Hastings Center
Garrison, NY 10524
(914) 424-4040
website: www.thehastingscenter.org

The center addresses fundamental ethical issues in health, medicine, and the environment, including euthanasia and physician-assisted suicide. It publishes a bimonthly journal, the *Hastings Center Report*, and other papers, some of which can be viewed on its website.

Hemlock Society
P.O. Box 101810, Denver, CO 80250-1810
(800) 247-7421 • fax: (303) 639-1224
e-mail: community@hemlock.org • website: www.hemlock.org

The Hemlock Society is the oldest, largest, and best known right-to-die organization in the United States. It works for increased choice in dying, including legalization of physician-assisted suicide, through lobbying, education, and patient advocacy. It provides educational material through its website; a quarterly newsletter, *TimeLines*; and brochures. Its website sells pamphlets, books, videos, and other material related to the right to die, such as "A Physician's View: Assisted Dying: A Moral and Ethical Choice" (pamphlet).

Human Life International
4 Family Life Ln., Front Royal, VA 22630
(540) 635-7884 • fax: (540) 636-7363
e-mail: hli@hli.org • website: www.hli.org

This Roman Catholic organization works to promote and defend the sanctity of life and family around the world. It believes that euthanasia and assisted suicide are morally unacceptable. HLI's publications include a monthly newsletter, *HLI Reports*. Its website sells audio tapes, booklets, and pamphlets on subjects including euthanasia such as "Imposed Death: What You Need to Know About Mercy Killing and Assisted Suicides" (booklet).

International Anti-Euthanasia Task Force
P.O. Box 760, Steubenville, OH 43952
(740) 282-3810
e-mail: info@iaetf.org • website: http://iaetf.org

This group opposes all forms of euthanasia. It tries to influence the public, legislators, and the courts to ban them. Its website includes a glossary, information about euthanasia-related court cases, and other resources. It offers or sells a variety of materials opposing euthanasia, includiing *Euthanasia: False Light* (video) and "Kevorkian" (fact sheet).

Last Acts Coalition
c/o Ms. Nancy Reller, Barksdale Ballard & Co.
1951 Kidwell Dr., Suite 205, Vienna, VA 22182
(703) 827-8771 • fax: (703) 827-0783
e-mail: nreller@bballard.com • website: www.lastacts.org

This coalition of health care organizations and others works to improve care of the dying as an alternative to physician-assisted suicide. It helps to arrange for speakers and other resources. Its website includes news releases, an electronic newsletter, and a page of links to other resources. It offers five brochures on "Loss and Grieving."

National Right to Life Committee
419 Seventh St. NW, Suite 500, Washington, DC 20004
(202) 626-8800
e-mail: nrlc@nrlc.org • website: www.nrlc.org

This organization opposes physician-assisted suicide and euthanasia as well as abortion and other threats to life. Its website includes press releases such as "The Netherlands Pursues Legalized Euthanasia."

Not Dead Yet
c/o Diane Coleman, Progress CIL, 7521 Madison St., Forest Park, IL 60130
(708) 209-1500 • fax: (708) 239-1735
website: www.notdeadyet.org

Not Dead Yet is a national grassroots disability rights organization. It opposes legalization of physician-assisted suicide and euthanasia because of risks it believes such actions present to disabled and chronically ill people. Its website includes materials such as the article "The REAL Hemlock Society" and a list of other disability rights organizations that oppose assisted suicide.

Partnership for Caring
1620 Eye Street NW, Suite 202, Washington, DC 20006
(800) 989-9455
website: www.partnershipforcaring.org

Partnership for Caring, formerly Choice in Dying, is a consumer movement dedicated to increasing Americans' awareness of the challenges and opportunities associated with life's end. It encourages people to fill out advance directives and discuss end-of-life issues. It publishes a quarterly newsletter and offers state-specific advance directive forms for a donation.

Project on Death in America
Open Society Institute, 400 W. 59th St., New York, NY 10019
(212) 548-0150
e-mail: pdia@sorosny.org • website: www.soros.org/death/index.htm

The project works to understand and transform the culture and experience of dying and bereavement through initiatives in research, scholarship, the humanities, and the arts. Through grants and other means it fosters innovation in the provision of care, public and professional education, and public policy. Its website provides access to research briefs, press releases, and a newsletter, which is issued at irregular intervals. Available materials include "New Research Examines Physicians' Experiences with the Oregon Death with Dignity Act" (research brief).

World Federation of Right to Die Societies
P.O. Box 570, Mill Valley, CA 94942
(415) 381-1573 • fax: (415) 381-1573
e-mail: jamison@aidindying.com • website: www.worldrtd.org

This international federation supports the right of the terminally ill to choose the time and manner of their death. It believes they should be able to ask for assistance in dying if necessary. It publishes a newsletter at irregular intervals, usually twice a year. In addition to the newsletter, its website offers news updates and a links page.

Bibliography

Books

Mark Blocher   *The Right to Die? Caring Alternatives to Euthanasia.* Chicago: Moody Press, 1999.

Seamus Cavan and Shean Dolan   *Euthanasia: The Debate over the Right to Die.* Brookshire, Texas: Rosen Publishing Group, 2000.

Paul Chamberlain   *Final Wishes: A Cautionary Tale on Death, Dignity and Physician-Assisted Suicide.* Downers Grove, Ill.: InterVarsity Press, 2000.

Edwin R. DuBose   *Physician Assisted Suicide: Religions and Public Policy Perspectives.* Chicago: Park Ridge Center for the Study of Health, Faith, and Ethics, 1999.

Gerald Dworkin, Sissela Bok, and R.G. Frey   *Euthanasia and Physician-Assisted Suicide (For and Against).* New York: Cambridge University Press, 1998.

Peter G. Filene   *In the Arms of Others: A Cultural History of the Right-to-Die in America.* Chicago: Ivan R. Dee, 1998.

Elaine Fox et al.   *Come Lovely and Soothing Death: The Right to Die Movement in the United States.* Farmington Hills, Mich.: Gale Group, 1999.

Derek Humphry and Mary Clement   *Freedom to Die: People, Politics and the Right-to-Die Movement.* New York: St. Martin's Press, 1998.

Edward J. Larson and Darrel W. Amundsen   *A Different Death: Euthanasia and the Christian Tradition.* Downers Grove, Ill.: InterVarsity Press, 1998.

David Mayo and Susan M. Wolf, eds.   *Physician-Assisted Suicide: Pro and Con.* Lanham, Md.: Rowman & Littlefield, 2000.

Charles F. McKhann   *A Time to Die: The Place for Physician Assistance.* New Haven, Conn.: Yale University Press, 1999.

Cedric A. Mims   *When We Die: The Science, Culture, and Rituals of Death.* New York: St. Martin's Press, 1999.

Robert Pool   *Negotiating a Good Death: Euthanasia in the Netherlands.* Binghamton, N.Y.: Haworth Press, 2000.

James D. Torr, ed.   *Opposing Viewpoints: Euthanasia.* San Diego, Calif.: Greenhaven Press, 2000.

Michael L. Uhlmann, ed.   *Last Rights: Assisted Suicide and Euthanasia Debated.* Grand Rapids, Mich.: William B. Eerdmans, 1998.

Melvin I. Urofsky   *Lethal Judgments: Assisted Suicide and American Law.* Lawrence: University Press of Kansas, 2000.

Sue Woodman   *Last Rights: The Struggle over the Right to Die.* New York: Plenum Press, 1998.

Lisa Yount   *Overview: Euthanasia.* San Diego, Calif.: Lucent Books, 2001.

Lisa Yount   *Library in a Book: Physician-Assisted Suicide and Euthanasia.* New York: Facts on File, 2000.

Marjorie B. Zucker   *The Right to Die Debate: A Documentary History.* Westport, Conn.: Greenwood Publishing Group, 1999.

Periodicals

Burke J. Balch   "Not Just Voluntary," *National Right to Life News*, June 10, 1999. Available from 419 7th St. NW, Suite 500, Washington, DC 20004.

Bruce Barcott   "Dale's Dilemma," *Life*, September 1, 1999.

Barry A. Bostrom   "Physician-Assisted Suicide: Reflections on Oregon's First Case," *National Right to Life News*, March 15, 1999.

Dan W. Brock   "A Critique of Three Objections to Physician-Assisted Suicide," *Ethics*, April 1999. Available from Department of Philosophy, Northwestern University, 1818 Hinman Ave., Evanston, IL 60208-1315.

Daniel Callahan   "Good Strategies and Bad: Opposing Physician-Assisted Suicide," *Commonweal*, December 3, 1999.

Courtney S. Campbell   "Give Me Liberty and Death: Assisted Suicide in Oregon," *The Christian Century*, May 5, 1999.

Melinda T. Derish   "Mature Minors Should Have the Right to Refuse Life-
and Kathleen   Sustaining Medical Treatment," *Journal of Law,*
Vanden Heuvel   *Medicine, and Ethics*, Summer 2000. Available from 765 Commonwealth Avenue, Suite 1634, Boston, MA 02215.

Richard M.   "A Dignified Death for the Suicide Agenda?" *National*
Doerflinger   *Right to Life News*, April 2000.

Ezekiel J. Emanuel   "The End of Euthanasia? Death's Door." *The New Republic*, May 17, 1999.

Ezekiel J. Emanuel   "What Is the Great Benefit of Legalizing Euthanasia or Physician-Assisted Suicide?" *Ethics*, April 1999.

Sherman Frankel   "The Dementia Dilemma," *Perspectives in Biology and Medicine*, Winter 1999. Available from 2715 North Charles St., Baltimore, MD 21218-4363.

Kevin P. Glynn   "'Double Effect': Getting the Argument Right," *Commonweal*, January 29, 1999.

John Guagliardo   "Kevorkian Case Focuses Attention on Terminal Illness," *McKnight's Long-Term Care News*, May 26, 1999. Available from Two Northfield Plaza, Suite 300, Northfield, IL 60093-1217.

Stephanie Gutmann   "Death and the Maiden," *The New Republic*, June 24, 1996.

Amy Haddad   "Ethics in Action," *RN*, March 2000. Available from Five Paragon Drive, Montvale, NJ 07645-1742.

Herbert Hendin — "Physician-Assisted Suicide: A Look at the Netherlands," *Current*, December 1997.

F.M. Kamm — "Physician-Assisted Suicide, the Doctrine of Double Effect, and the Ground of Value," *Ethics*, April 1999.

John F. Kavenaugh — "Killing and Letting Die," *America*, September 23, 2000.

David B. McCurdy — "Saying What We Mean: The Redefining of Euthanasia," *The Christian Century*, July 17, 1996.

David Miller — "From Life to Death in a Peaceful Instant," *The Humanist*, May 2000.

Pamela J. Miller — "Life After Death with Dignity: The Oregon Experience," *Social Work*, May 2000. Available from 750 First Street NE, Suite 700, Washington, DC 20002-4241.

Richard H. Nicholson — "No Painless Death Yet for European Euthanasia Debate," *Hastings Center Report*, May 2000. Available from Hastings Center, Garrison, NY 10524.

David Orentlicher and Arthur Caplan — "The Pain Relief Promotion Act of 1999: A Serious Threat to Palliative Care," *Journal of the American Medical Association*, January 12, 2000. Available from 515 N. State Street, Chicago, IL 60610.

Jennifer A. Parks — "Why Gender Matters to the Euthanasia Debate," *Hastings Center Report*, January 2000.

Albert W. Preston and Thomas Preston — "Facing Death on Your Own Terms," *Newsweek*, May 22, 2000.

Claire Rayner — "You Say Murder, I Say Euthanasia," *New Statesman*, June 19, 2000.

Tania Salem — "Physician-Assisted Suicide," *Hastings Center Report*, May 1999.

Thomas A. Shannon — "Physician-Assisted Suicide: Ten Questions," *Commonweal*, June 1, 1996.

Joseph P. Shapiro — "Euthanasia's Home," *U.S. News and World Report*, January 13, 1997.

William Swanson — "Mortal Concern," *Minneapolis–St. Paul Magazine*, October 1996. Available from 220 S. Sixth Street, Minneapolis, MN 55402.

Judith Jarvis Thomson — "Physician-Assisted Suicide: Two Moral Arguments," *Ethics*, April 1999.

Liz Townsend — "British Health Service Doctors Accused of Involuntary Euthanasia," *National Right to Life News*, June 2000.

J. David Velleman — "A Right of Self-Determination?" *Ethics*, April 1999.

Walter Wright — "Historical Analogies, Slippery Slopes, and the Question of Euthanasia," *Journal of Law, Medicine, and Ethics*, Summer 2000.

INDEX